The Timekeeper

Catherine Twomey Fosnot

New Perspectives on Learning, LLC
1194 Ocean Avenue
New London, CT 06320

Copyright © 2019 Catherine Twomey Fosnot

ISBN-13: 978-1-7335321-1-2

THE TIMEKEEPERS

Table of Contents

Students are introduced to the idea of measuring time. They try counting first and realize some number words take longer say and there are problems when they try to compare durations. The need for constant intervals is solved with a timer that keeps track of seconds and students work in pairs doing movement activities for 30 seconds trying to estimate when the time is up.

After a discussion on the challenges of estimating 30 seconds, students return to work to try one more time to estimate 30 seconds while moving, culminating with the making of a poster for a subsequent gallery walk and congress. The focus of the congress is on measuring, marking, and determining time differences on duration bars.

A minilesson on splitting a rectangular bar into fourths and halves to mark minutes and seconds serves as a foundation for a new investigation: how long is a minute? Students continue the estimating work done on Day One and Two, but with a minute as a new duration. They realize the longer the duration the harder it is to estimate the time and then learn about some other timekeepers that can be helpful—digital and analog clocks.

The analog clock is introduced in a minilesson, and students learn about hours and how 60 minutes equals one hour. With partners, they anticipate what they will likely be doing at each hour and half hour throughout the day and fill out a schedule for the day.

After a minilesson using more analog clock images, a matching game is introduced using cards with digital and analog clock faces. Math workshop ends with the making of a learning scroll— a documentation of the learning and the activities that occurred over the duration of the unit.

Unit Overview

The focus of this unit is the extension of linear measurement to the measurement of time. Time is continuous; it flows. But when durations of time are measured (the cake needs to bake for 40 minutes), there are beginnings and endpoints to focus on. Some durations are long; others are short. To compare durations, standard units are needed like hours, minutes, and seconds and these can be decomposed, added, seen as fractional pieces of a larger unit (for example, half an hour), or exchanged—for example, 30 minutes can be exchanged for half an hour. The teaching of time has often been misconstrued as the "telling of time." Being able to read and recite time from the face of the clock does not mean that children understand time, the passing of it, or the mathematics involved in the measuring of it. This unit is crafted and sequenced carefully to foster those understandings.

The unit is designed to align with the CCSS Standards of Practice and the following core objectives:

Tell and write time.

CCSS.MATH.CONTENT.1.MD.B.3

Tell and write time in hours and half-hours using analog and digital clocks.

Reason with shapes and their attributes.

CCSS.MATH.CONTENT.1.G.A.3

Partition circles and rectangles into two and four equal shares, describe the shares using the words *halves*, *fourths*, and *quarters*, and use the phrases *half of*, *fourth of*, and *quarter of*. Describe the whole as two of, or four of the shares. Understand for these examples that decomposing into more equal shares creates smaller shares.

The Mathematical Landscape

What are young children's conceptions of time and how do they experience it? According to Piaget (2007, originally published in 1970), up until around the ages of 7 or 8, children are unable to evaluate time durations accurately. His early studies showed that young children's time judgements were context-dependent and closely bound up with the situation within which time was experienced. For example, they confused the difficulty of a task (such as putting lead disks vs. wooden disks in a bin) with time duration. Although the durations were the same, children believed that it took them longer to do the heavy ones. Similar results were found by other researchers. When looking at a bright light versus a dim one (both on for the same duration), young children stated the bright light was on longer, evidence that they were confounding intensity of the light with time (Arlin 1989).

Current research, however, shows that the development of an understanding of time is much more complex than first thought. It turns out that even 6-month-old infants can discriminate two durations if the ratio of the durations is greater than a 1:2 (Brannon et al. 2007). Younger infants with even more limited capacities can discriminate different durations. During a training phase infants were presented with two sounds, one short (½ second) and one longer (1½ seconds). They were trained to look to the left after the short sound and to the right after the longer sound. In the later test phase, they were also presented with intermediate durations. The longer the sounds, the longer babies looked to the right (Provasi et al. 2010). In another study, children between the ages of 2-5 years were able to space their responses by a given time duration in order to make slides appear on a screen, and their ability to do so increased when they had to perform motor activities during the waiting period (Droit et al. 1990). Keeping children's attention focused on the passage of time raises their ability to discriminate and estimate durations. The higher the child's attention/concentration score, the better their sensitivity to time. This may explain why time duration estimation is often impaired in children with ADHD.

Time is continuous; it flows. And yet, humans over eons of years have found ways to mathematize it. We measure it in iterated chunks as if it weren't continuously flowing. We decompose our invented measurement chunks (like days) into hours, minutes, and seconds, and even into fractional units when we talk about half hours and half minutes. We interchange equivalent pieces, calling 30 minutes half an hour, or 1800 seconds; two-thirty is described as 2 hours and 30 minutes, as half-past two, and as 2½ hours. To make matters worse, as teachers we must ensure our young students can read, write, and understand both digital and analog mathematical representations of this continuous pure scientific phenomenon we call time, and do it with meaning!

Historically, time has been taught in our schools as a reading and drawing activity, rather than as a math activity. The focus has been on "telling time" (reading it off a clock) and rendering a given time with a drawing of the clock's hands. Reading hands on a clock makes little sense to a child who has yet to construct the meaning of the measurement units and the durations they represent. This is as non-sensical as trying to teach a child about number by engaging him in the reading and writing of numerals and disregarding an understanding of cardinality. To help children understand time as measured durations, teachers have often used calendar activities, the counting of days in school, and the celebrating the 100th day. These activities have little to no effect on developing an understanding of the measurement of time because the durations are not continuous, and they are too long and erratic in duration. A day in school to a young child is removed from the continuous flow of time and removed even from the benefits of measuring time, as one cannot stay focused for that long a period to understand what is being measured. During the day there are many, many distractions to get a sense of the duration, and the lengths of children's days can vary. Some days feel very long, and some are experienced as very short, depending on the activities being done. Some days are actually even half days—days with early dismissals. Yet, they are all counted as a day in school.

The mathematics ideas and strategies we use to measure time should not be thought of as just a rote list of skills to explain and practice. Telling and writing time in hours and half-hours with meaning using analog and digital clocks is an outcome of a long progressive journey of development comprised of several big ideas, strategies, and models.

The Timekeepers is a serious attempt to make use of the research on children's notions of time and the progressive development of an understanding of the mathematics involved in the measurement of time. As you work through this unit there are several big ideas, strategies, and models on the landscape to encourage and celebrate. Figure 1 depicts the landmarks of development that you will likely see your students developing as you progress through this unit. A description of each follows.

A more complete landscape of the measurement of time is provided on page 12 so that you can situate the development you will likely see with this unit, on the longer journey your students will travel as they develop a deeper understanding in the years to come.

The Landscape of Learning

BIG IDEAS

- ❖ Durations of time can be compared
- ❖ Discrete Degrees
- ❖ Variations
- ❖ Transitivity
- ❖ Durations of time can be measured
- ❖ To compare durations a standard unit is needed
- ❖ Grouping: larger units can encompass (and be decomposed into) smaller units
- ❖ Part/whole: durations can be added and subtracted
- ❖ Durations can be cut into equal (fractional) portions
- ❖ Unitizing and place value

STRATEGIES

- ❖ Uses only discrete labels
- ❖ Uses comparative labels
- ❖ Measures and compares durations by counting
- ❖ Ratio mapping
- ❖ Uses standard units
- ❖ Uses addition and decomposition to determine overall duration
- ❖ Uses subtraction to determine how much more time is needed
- ❖ Substitutes an equivalent expression

MODELS

- ❖ Bar Model
- ❖ Timer
- ❖ Digital Clock
- ❖ Analog Clock

Figure 1

As young children explore the investigations within this unit, several big ideas arise. These include:

Durations of time can be compared

One of the first big ideas that young children construct about time is that it can be an attribute to characterize the durations of two sounds, or the time interval between two events. Even as infants they can differentiate long durations from short durations, particularly when the ratio of the durations being compared is at least 2:1. Some researchers even suggest that this ability may be innate and based on a neurological internal time clock. Brackbill and Fitzgerald (1972) showed that one month old infants could discern short time intervals. After being conditioned to light changes occurring every 20 seconds, the pupils of the eyes of the infants continued to contract every 20 seconds even when the lights were stopped!

Discrete Degrees

In the preschool years, as children attempt to describe time differences, they often have only two categories: long and short. Some things take a really long time, like a long car ride (will we ever get there?), and other durations are short, like eating an ice cream cone (mine went too fast, I want more). Since we know from research that infants can discern and compare durations, it is most likely more of a focus issue and the lack of clarity on the beginning and endpoints of the durations. When the magnitude of the differences in durations is great, young children can sort the durations into two categories. But slighter variations become difficult to discern for youngsters, particularly if they are distracted.

Variations

Eventually discrete labels become insufficient and as their brains mature, children become better able to focus. They need a way to describe subtle variations in order to compare (Forman and Hill, 1984). At first, they may talk about a little-long, a really long, and a really, really long time—still discrete labels. But eventually these words, too, become insufficient and young children start using comparative terms to describe the variations they see. For example, they might say one way takes long*er* than another. Understanding that times can vary brings about a desire to measure time. At first children may count. Think of how young children play hide-and-seek. They cover their eyes as other players hide and count faster, or not as long, and they know this will bring cries of, "You did not give enough time!"

Transitivity

Eventually, comparison opens a new door: a possibility to use a third external object to compare and order durations and the logic of transitivity is constructed (If *a>b, and b>c, then a>c*). This is a critical big idea in the development of measurement. The ability to use a third object (such as a timer) to determine which of three events was longer and to order them requires the logic of transitivity.

Durations of time can be measured

As children attempt to unite their understanding of number and their understanding of linear measurement to time, they often first employ their knowledge of cardinality to measure time: they count.

They may also count faster at times and slower at other times and it may not at first matter to them that some words have more syllables and take longer to say.

To compare durations a standard unit is needed

When two people count at different speeds and some words take longer to say, different answers result, and these issues can begin to create disequilibrium to an earlier scheme based on cardinality. These problems bring children to eventually construct the idea that it is important to measure with constant intervals, which an external device, like a timer, can provide.

Grouping: larger units can encompass (and be decomposed into) smaller units

Grouping is an idea that is developed as an extension of the earlier idea of using standard units. Iterated smaller units (like seconds) can be grouped into minutes, which in turn can be grouped into hours. As children come to realize that if larger units are used, the total number of units needed is smaller, they can more appropriately choose a unit to use to measure a duration. For example, short durations would be best to measure in seconds; and longer durations might be best measured in hours and minutes. Very long durations might be measured in days or years.

Part/whole: durations can be added and subtracted

It is the integration of the smaller units with the whole into a part/whole structure that supports children to come to realize that lengths of time can be added and subtracted. Now they can add on and use several addition and subtraction strategies they may have developed. For example, now they can defend why the difference between two durations can be determined by adding on or subtracting.

Durations can be cut into equal (fractional) portions

Once grouping is constructed, decomposing is on the near horizon. It is not a large step to consider how, if time durations can be added and subtracted, a duration can also be decomposed. As children work with clocks and are exposed to the turning of the hands around a circle, and as they explore cutting rectangles and circles into equal pieces, they develop an early understanding of halves and fourths. This allows them to consider how an hour can be cut into half hours. Children are also helped by their knowledge of cardinality, and in particular their knowledge of doubles. Understanding that 30 + 30 = 60, helps them come to understand that 30 minutes is equal to a half hour. And then, as they get older they become more flexible in seeing 15 minutes as a quarter of an hour, or as 3 groups of five minutes.

Unitizing and place value

At first children may think that a timer should register 60 seconds (after 59 seconds) instead of a minute. They expect it should say 00:60 first and then go to 01:00 next, and they can be quite surprised to see that the counter goes from 00:59 to 01:00. They understand that 60 seconds makes a minute but coming to deeply understand that one notation can be substituted for another is quite another story. It requires unitizing the 60 seconds into a new unit and shifting it a place! This is a huge cognitive leap akin to deeply understanding place value. The new value (1 minute) is represented in a new place, replacing 60 seconds.

As you work with the activities in this unit, you will notice that students will use many strategies to solve the problems that are posed to them. Here are some strategies to notice:

Uses only discrete labels

Preschool children often use words like long, or short, but only as *discrete* labels. They do not use comparative words like longer, or shorter.

Uses comparative labels

Children's language about time changes as they compare and come to understand that there are variations along a continuum. They now talk about some things taking longer than others and they can order durations. Note the use of the comparative suffix—longer, instead of long.

Measures and compares durations by counting

Children will often count to measure time. They pause when they forget what number comes next and some numbers take longer to say than others because of the number of syllables in the words. And they may not see a problem with this! When you see this strategy, it is very important to bring it up for discussion and ask students to consider if it matters. It is precisely a well-facilitated discussion on this strategy that will support the development of an understanding of measurement as iterated standard units, iterated constant intervals covering a timespan, point to point.

Ratio-preserving mapping

As children begin to compare and represent time durations, you may see them using gestures to show the relative measurements in comparison to each other. For example, they preserve the ratio trying to use their arm span to show how one time period is twice as long as another.

Uses standard units

Once children construct the idea that the intervals of the count need to be regular, that pausing between counts and using longer words matter, they come to the realization that a standard unit is necessary for reliable measurement comparisons. When they learn of timers, they use them with meaning.

Uses addition and decomposition to determine overall duration

Whereas children determined length of time earlier by counting (or having the timer keep track) of individual units, they now use addition. If an hour has passed and then 30 seconds more, they add the pieces saying it took one hour and 30 seconds, or 1 hour and a half.

Uses subtraction to determine how much more time is needed

Subtraction is used to calculate the measurement of missing pieces. For example, if a total duration is known (2 hours), as well as a given duration (1½ hours), subtraction (or adding on to find the missing addend) is used to determine the length of the missing unknown section. In later grades, this strategy develops into several flexible strategies for calculating elapsed time.

Substitutes an equivalent expression

An important strategy for measurement to notice is when a child exchanges one numeric expression for an equivalent one. For example, a child might say 30 seconds is half a minute, or 60 seconds is a minute, knowing one can be exchanged for the other. This is an early algebraic strategy!

MATHEMATICAL MODELING

Model of a situation

Initially models emerge as a representation *of* a situation; later they are used by teachers to represent children's computation strategies. Ultimately they are appropriated by children as powerful tools *for* thinking (Gravemeijer 1999). As you progress through this unit, your children will engage in estimating time and comparing how close they came to the goal of 30 seconds. Their estimates are placed on duration bars which are eventually used to compare durations and represent equivalent durations (for example 60 seconds to a minute). The model encourages a linear representation of number and operation for children that is powerful for developing mental arithmetic strategies (Beishuizen 1993; Klein, Beishuizen, and Treffers 2002). Comparing time differences this way unites ideas of distance and duration with quantity and is a precursor to the model of a timeline.

Model of Student Strategies

Children benefit from seeing the teacher model their strategies on duration bars. Once the model has been introduced as a representation of the situation, you can use it to model children's addition and subtraction strategies as they work to determine differences in durations.

Model as a Tool for Thinking

Eventually children are introduced to timekeeping devices: timers keeping track of seconds and minutes, and digital and analog clocks keeping track of hours and minutes. These are now used as tools for measuring time externally and serve as tools for thinking.

A graphic of the full landscape of learning for this unit is provided on page 12. The purpose of the graphic is to allow you to see the longer journey of students' development and to place your work with this unit within the scope of this long-term development. You may also find the graphic helpful as a way to record the progress of individual students for yourself. Each landmark can be shaded in as you find evidence in a student's work and in what the student says—evidence that a landmark strategy, big idea, or way of modeling has been constructed. Or, you may prefer to use our web-based app (www.NewPerspectivesOnAssessment.com) to document your children's growth digitally. In a sense, you will be recording the individual pathways your students take as they develop as young mathematicians.

References and Resources

Arlin, M. (1989). The effect of physical work, mental work, and quantity on children's time perception. *Perception and Psychophysics*, 45 (3) 209-214.

Beishuizen, Meindert (1993). Mental strategies and materials or models for addition and subtraction up to 100 in Dutch second grades. *Journal for Research in Mathematics Education,* 24, 294–323.

Brackbill, Yvonne and Hiram E. Fitzgerald (1972). Stereotype Temporal Conditioning in Infants. *Psychophysiology.* 9 (6), 569-577.

Brannon, E.M., Suand, S, and Libertus, K. (2007) Temporal discrimination increases in precision over development and parallels in the development of numerosity discrimination. *Developmental Science* 10, 6, 770-777.

Droit, S., Pouthas, V., and Jacquet, A.Y. (1990) Temporal learning in 4½ - 6-year-old children. *Journal of Experimental Child Psychology.* 50 , 305-321.

Gravemeijer, Koeno (1999). How emergent models may foster the constitution of formal mathematics. *Mathematical Thinking and Learning 1* (2): 155–77.

Hill, Fleet and George E. Forman (1984). *Constructive Play.* NY: Abel.

Klein, Anton S., Meindert Beishuizen, and Adri Treffers (2002). The empty number line in Dutch second grade, In *Lessons Learned from Research,* eds. Judith Sowder and Bonnie Schapelle. Reston, VA: NCTM.

Piaget, Jean (2007, original version 1970). *The Child's Conception of Time.* Oxfordshire, London: Routledge.

Provasi, J., Rattat, A.C. and Droit-Volet, S. (2010). Temporal bisection on 4-month-old infants. *Journal of Experimental Psychology: Animal Behavior Processes.* 37 (1), 108-113.

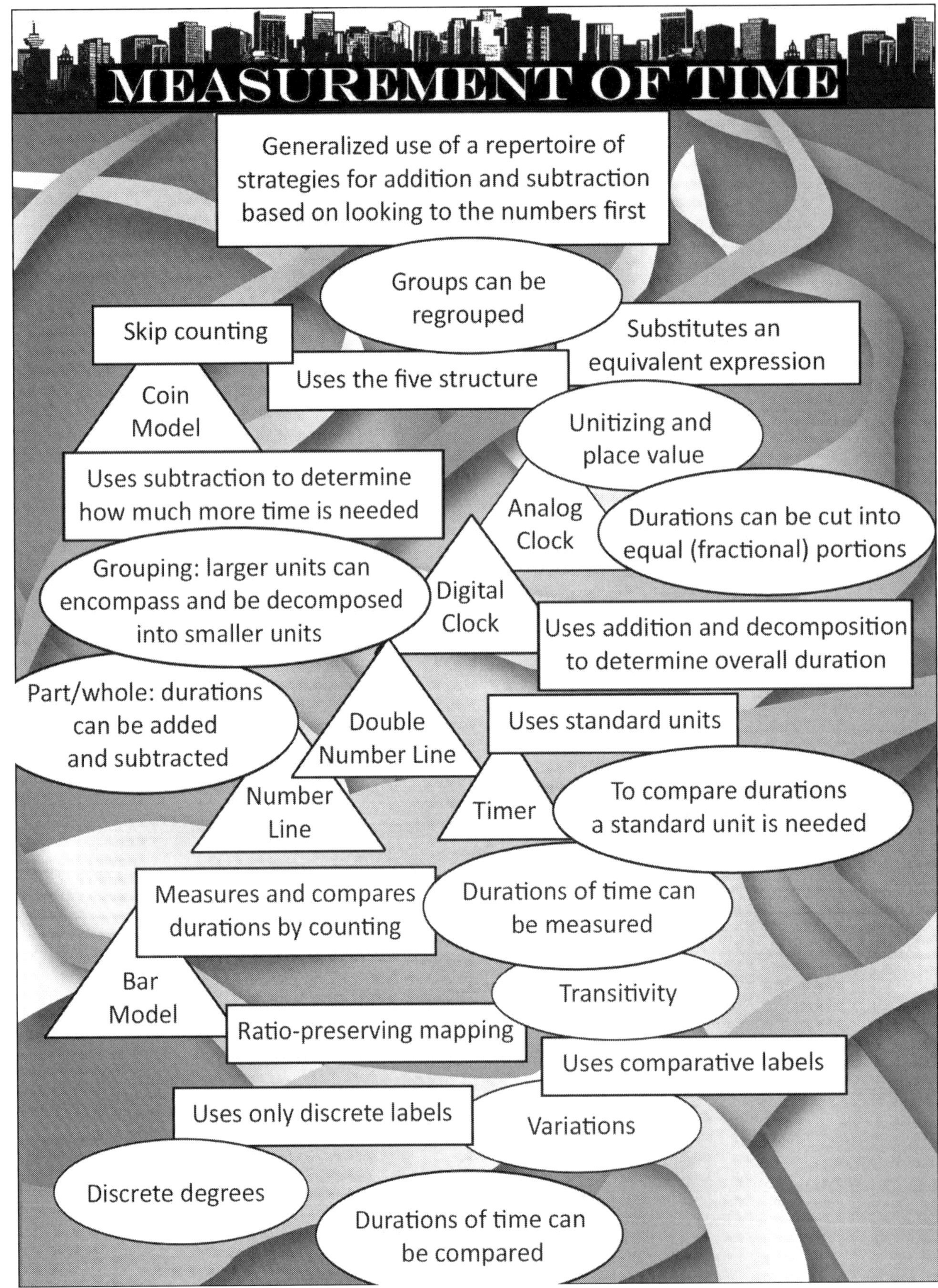

The Landscape of Learning: measurement of time on the horizon showing landmark strategies (rectangles), big ideas (ovals), and models (triangles).

DAY ONE

WHAT IS TIME?

The unit begins with the reading of a portion of the story *The Timekeepers* (Appendix A). Children subsequently work in pairs and engage in two short movement activities, keeping track of the duration of each with timers. The durations are represented and compared as marked lengths on duration bars and differences are explored.

Day One Outline

Developing the Context

❖ Introduce the context of time by reading *The Timekeepers* (Appendix A, up to page 40.)

❖ Measuring with a timer, have a child estimate 30 seconds while doing a sustained movement activity (such as standing, jumping up and down, or waving arms) and to stop when she thinks the time is up. When she stops, show the timer and report the actual time duration.

❖ Mark the end of a length of 30 connecting cubes and the actual duration on a strip of adding machine paper. Provide discussion on how close the student's estimation of time was.

❖ Repeat with a second child. Foster discussion on how the two attempts at estimating 30 seconds in duration compare. Send pairs off with materials to make further attempts at estimating, representing, and comparing.

Supporting the Investigation

❖ As students work, move around and confer. Encourage students to note how close they come to 30 seconds and to share their strategies. Support them to measure with the cubes and mark the lengths on the strip of adding machine paper.

Math Journals

❖ Provide time to reflect and articulate learning from the day.

Materials Needed

The Timekeepers (Appendix A)

Small Timers showing seconds and minutes (one per pair of students)

Connecting cubes (60 per pair, sorted into two colors, 30 of each color).

Strips of adding machine paper (one per pair of students, approximately 2 meters long.

Scissors

Math Journals

Pencils

Developing the Context

Read the first part of the story *The Timekeepers* (Appendix A), stopping at the mark on page 40. Explain that you have a timer, too, and invite a child to do a sustained movement activity (such as standing, jumping, waving arms) and to stop when he thinks the time is up. Use a timer that counts up and when he stops, show the timer and report the actual time duration.

Mark the end of a length of 30 connecting cubes (made by alternating groups of 5 red and 5 white cubes) on a strip of adding machine paper (cut approximately 2 meters long), as shown in Figure 3. Then, using the cubes again (and adding more if needed), mark the actual duration. Provide discussion on how close the student's estimation of time was.

30

Figure 3: Marking the intended elapsed time

Repeat with a second child. Foster discussion on how the two attempts at estimating 30 seconds in duration compare.

Form partnerships and invite students to see how close they can come to estimating how long 30 seconds is. Send pairs off with small timers, cubes, strips of adding machine paper, journals, and pencils.

> ### Tech tip:
>
> Colorful versions of the appendices for this unit that you can display as you read the story are available on www.NewPerspectivesOnline.net.
>
> An online search will also provide you with several free digital versions of timers that you can use as you develop the context. Just make sure you use one that keeps track of elapsed time by counting up. Don't use a stopwatch or the type of timer that you have to set beforehand that then counts down to zero. Using the latter timekeeping device requires subtraction when determining the duration of the child's activity because the elapsed time is unknown until the activity ends. Understanding why subtraction is needed in this context can be difficult for most first graders to understand.

Supporting the Investigation

Let students get settled and ensure everyone understands the goal of the investigation. Then listen in on some conversations. Here are some strategies and big ideas you are likely to see emerging:

❖ Most students will likely count to 30 as they move. If they have chosen an activity that requires some concentration (for example hand-waving) they will likely struggle with the multi-tasking of moving and counting simultaneously. They will likely go slower, also, as the numbers become greater, because saying twenty-seven, for example, takes longer than saying one or two; it's 4 syllables, rather than one, and thus saying the number will likely take 4 times as long. Let children experience this for themselves before reminding them of what Elijah said in the story. One of the big ideas they will need to construct is that measurement of time is done with constant intervals that can be iterated. Repeating a standard unit is needed in order to compare durations reliably.

❖ Some students may choose an activity (such as handclapping or tapping a foot) that allows them to have a regular beat. This strategy may bring them closer to judging 30 seconds, and it shows an emerging understanding of the need for a consistent, standard unit. As they work they will need to consider how long a second is and will be gaining a sense of a 30-second duration.

❖ Note what students do to represent the time duration on the strip using a length of cubes. Often they move the length of cubes as they work, and the length slips off the beginning point. As you confer, ask students if this slippage matters and support them to see that if the starting place isn't carefully taken into consideration the mark for the overall length gets put in the wrong place.

❖ Other students may count to 10 three times as a way to keep the beat regular and may also use lengths of ten cubes repeatedly when measuring where to put the marks on the strip. Note also how students make use of the two colors. Some may use alternating groups of 5 or 10. This is very nice and shows that five and ten can be prioritized. As you confer, ask them if pieces of time can be added. Note the big ideas that underlie this strategy related to a part/whole relations and support discussion on them: (1) time can be measured with small units, or bigger units (3 sections of 10 units each are equal to 30 individual units...as students begin to work with analog clocks later in the unit, this idea will return as they explore how the hour and half-hour can be measured in minutes); (2) units of time can be added or subtracted (if one duration is 27 seconds and the intended duration is 30 seconds, 3 more seconds are needed).

Inside One Classroom: Conferring with Students at Work

James (the teacher): I'm so interested in the strategy that you are working on. May I sit and confer with you? It looks like you are counting to 10 while you are standing, and that you are keeping track of the number of times you do that. Am I right?

Sydney: (smiling) Yes.

Jessie: We are counting to ten, so we don't have to say any long numbers.

James: Oh, what a good idea! Just like Elijah said in the story! You are making the units you measure with a similar size. That's important, isn't it. It looks like you used two color of cubes, too? Tell me about that.

Sydney: Well, we thought if we made towers of ten in different colors we could skipcount, like 10, 20, 30.

James: Wow! What a great way to think about it! Another good idea. You two are cooking with full burners today (smiling)! When you lined up your towers of ten, you left a little bit of a gap between them, and I see that this first

Author's notes

As James confers, notice how he starts the conferral by listening and getting clarification and then he celebrates the approach. After clarifying and celebrating, he probes to generate conversation on whether finding the exact starting point matters – do gaps matter when measuring?

tower has slid off the starting point a bit. Does this matter?

Jessie: Maybe. Oh yeah, it does. If we leave gaps Sydney, it will be longer.

James: What do you think, Sydney? Is Jessie right? Is it really not 30 units long if you leave gaps, or if you are not careful and it slips off the starting point? *(Jessie starts fixing the towers by snapping the tens together, but not alternating the colors).*

Sydney: *(Pondering at first).* Yes. But I think you should do red, white, red.....not red, red, white.

James: What do you think, Jessie? Would that help you see the tens better?

Jessie: *(Pondering but then grinning).* Oh yeah!

James: So how close did you come trying to estimate 30 seconds? Was this a good strategy, or not?

Sydney: Pretty close. We got 34. See, 10, 20, 30, and 4 more.

James: Hmmm....So do you think your counts were too slow, or too fast? *(Both students are now pondering the question. Jessie says, "too slow" and Sydney says, "too fast.")* Hmmm...which is it? Sydney, tell us why you think "too fast."

Sydney: *(shrugs).* I just think so. Jessie counted fast.

Jessie: I think I went too slow. I went slower than the timer. That's why it took me longer to get to 30. If you go too slow, it takes longer. I counted to 30, but the timer said it was 34 seconds. I went slower than the timer.

James: I think I hear you saying something big here. Are you saying that if we are measuring time with seconds, but using counting to estimate, if we count too slow or too fast, it changes what we get? I'm going to let you both think about this, because I need to get to another group? But experiment, and let me know, OK? Because I think this will be an important idea to discuss in our congress tomorrow.

Note how James goes back and forth between his two students to ensure the conversation does not become a dialogue between him and one student. He engages both students in the conversation.

James asks a powerful question here. His question focuses the students on another big idea: the size of the unit (the speed of counting) affects the value. This big idea supports the need to use a device to keep time—one that uses a standard measure, like seconds and minutes.

James celebrates what the students have done. Then he leaves them to think. They have hit on something big. By going off he provides them with reflection time to consider the importance of using a consistent, standard, measurement unit.

Math Journals

During the last five minutes of class, ask students to write in their math journals about the big "a-ha" moments or discoveries they had today. Taking the time to reflect will help them hold on to their ideas, expose areas of confusion, and set the stage for tomorrow's work. Reading these entries will help you, the teacher, see where each student is on the landscape of learning. Towards that aim, ask students,

> *"Before we end for today, write about your latest thinking using words and pictures so that you can hold on to it and remember. How close did you come? Draw a picture of your bars and the marks you made. Were you surprised to see how long 30 seconds is? What are the big ideas you are working on? I will read what you wrote and write back to you."*

Before the next class, read the entries and respond to each mathematician at least briefly with a question or prompt to strengthen or challenge thinking. Use the strategies and big ideas on the landscape of learning described in the Overview section of the unit as a guide.

Reflections on the Day

Today, students worked as "timekeepers" trying to estimate 30 seconds. Doing so gave them opportunities to consider time as a duration that can be measured. They also discussed comparisons of durations and this brought up the idea that duration times can be added and subtracted. Familiarity with 30 seconds (half a minute) will affect their developing sense of time and ways to measure it. Note the many ideas and strategies you witnessed emerging today and think about the gallery walk and math congress that you will hold tomorrow. Which strategies and ideas would be powerful to discuss? How did students compare differences in the durations? Did they count on, count backwards, or make use of tens? What big ideas about measurement of time emerged? Did any students discuss the importance of a consistent, regular beat or interval in order to compare two durations and how the timer provides a standard unit? Which posters will you use, and in which order, to ensure a rich, growth-producing conversation for everyone?

DAY TWO

ESTIMATING AND MEASURING 30 SECONDS

Today begins with students reading their math journals and noting the comments and entries you made as you reflected on what they wrote at the end of math workshop yesterday. Then students return to work to try one more time to estimate 30 seconds while moving, culminating with the making of a poster for a subsequent gallery walk and congress. The focus of the congress is on measuring, marking, and determining time differences.

Day Two Outline

Math Journals

❖ Provide quiet time with math journals for students to read the comments they have received and to revisit their own reflections from the previous day. If needed help them to read your responses.

❖ Journals will be used again after the math congress.

Facilitating the Gallery Walk

❖ Have students try to estimate 30 seconds one more time and make a poster.

❖ Confer with children as they put finishing touches to their posters, asking them to consider the most important things they want to tell their audience.

❖ Conduct a gallery walk to allow students time to reflect and comment on each other's posters.

Facilitating the Math Congress

❖ Convene students at the meeting area to discuss a few important ideas they noticed about measuring and estimating time and to discuss strategies they used to determine how close they came to 30 seconds, specifically the time differences.

Materials Needed

Students' work from Day One

Lined sticky notes, several per student

Small Timers showing seconds (one per pair of students)

Connecting cubes (60 per pair, sorted into two colors, 30 of each color).

Strips of adding machine paper (one per pair of students, approximately 2 meters (or yards) long.

Scissors

Math Journals

Poster paper

Glue sticks

Markers and Pencils

Math Journals

Provide students with about 5 minutes to read over your responses to their journal entries from Day One. Move around and help them read your comments as needed. Ask them to write back to you if they wish, as doing so sets the expectation that journal writing in math is important and should be taken seriously. This time will also prepare them to return to their work if they are not yet finished. Then have them return to work and try to estimate 30 seconds one more time, trying again to get as close as they can to 30 seconds. As they finish, pass out chart paper, markers, and glue sticks and invite them to work on posters for a gallery and congress.

Facilitating the Gallery Walk

As students work on posters, move around and confer asking them to consider the most important things they want to tell their audience and reminding them that it is important to explain or show how they determined the difference in the measurements. For example, they might use an open number line to show the strip and mark it, and then add numbers to show the difference between the marks. Support the use of invented spelling, just as you do in writer's workshop.

After a sufficient amount of time, have students display their posters in the classroom for their peers to view. If students have used drawing paper, you can display the posters around the room or on tables. Posters might also be displayed on easels or taped to a whiteboard. Once all the groups have placed their posters up for display, explain to your students that during a gallery walk they will walk around and look at the other posters. They will have an important job: reading to try to understand what another group was showing on their poster. Explain to students that they will walk silently around reading the posters. As they walk around they should be thinking about questions like, "Do I understand this?" "Is this like what I did on my poster?" "Is this strategy like mine?" "Am I confused about a part?" and "Do I disagree?"

Depending on the writing level of your students, you may wish to give your students blank post-it notes so that they can draw or write their ideas, or you may wish to provide them with the following pre-made sticky notes:

✓ **Check Mark:** I really understand this.
? **Question Mark:** I wonder about this, or I have a question here.
⇄ **Connection sign:** I agree. I did the same thing on my poster.

Have students walk around and read a few of the posters silently for 5-10 minutes. Tell them they do not have to read every poster. Just make sure that every poster gets read by at least a few children and that every poster gets at least a few sticky notes.

After the gallery walk, you can invite the groups to go back to their posters to see what comments were left. By having this gallery walk, you are encouraging your students to reflect and comment on written and visual forms of mathematics—something professional mathematicians do! They are learning to write and read a viable argument, one of the CCSS Standards of Mathematical Practice.

During the gallery walk it's important that you make comments on posters as well, so that students see you as a member of the community who is really interested in their thinking. Look for moments and places where you can show your students that you are seriously trying to understand their thinking and remember, you are their mentor. Appreciate their good thinking, comment on interesting approaches, and suggest where more detail could be helpful to support understanding. Raise questions that might push for generalization or further insights. As you move around, look for big ideas and strategies from the landscape. This will help you to plan which pieces of work you will select for the congress, if you haven't done that already.

Facilitating the Math Congress

Review the posters and choose a few that you can use for a discussion that will deepen understanding and support growth along the landscape of learning described in the Overview. There is not necessarily one best plan for a congress. There are many different plans that might all be supportive of development. You'll want to focus the congress on what affected a good estimate such as: (1) counting too slow, or too fast; (2) how difficult the task was and why a standard unit of measure (like seconds on a timer) is important to know how long something took; and (3) the computation strategies students used to calculate the differences in estimates.

<table>
<tr><td colspan="2" align="center">Inside One Classroom: A Portion of the Math Congress</td></tr>
<tr><td>

James (the teacher): Jessie and Sydney, yesterday when I conferred with you, you were having a great conversation about your estimate when you got 34. Come tell us what happened.

Jessie: I was trying to get to 30 seconds, so I counted to 30, but the timer said 34 when I stopped. Sydney said I went too fast, but I think I went too slow. That's why the timer said 34 when I stopped.

James: What might have made your counting slow? Why is that? Does anyone know?

Sydney: I think you went too fast. You got up to 34, when the timer only got to 30.

James: How many of you got a number bigger than 30, like Jessie? (*Most hands go up*). How many of you got numbers smaller than 30? (*Two hands go up*). Let's turn and talk with an elbow partner about this. If your estimate was a number bigger than 30, did you count too fast, or too slow? (*A real buzz starts, with spirited disagreement. James moves around and listens in on several conversations and then*

</td><td>

Author's notes

James chooses to start the congress with a discussion by Jessie and Sydney. A conversation like this will be beneficial for all and will bring up the idea of the need for a constant interval.

James provides pair talk here to heighten reflection.

</td></tr>
</table>

resumes whole group discussion). Did anyone have a helpful partner? Sydney?	*Asking if anyone had a helpful partner implicitly sends the message that pair talk needs to be accountable talk.*
Sydney: Jessie convinced me. I forgot the timer said 34. 34 is more than 30, so Jessie went longer than 30 seconds.	
James: Wow! Put your hand up if you understand what Sydney means. (*Several hands go up but not all.*) Tammy, what did you and Ben decide?	
Tammy: We're not sure. We got 40 and we counted, too.	
James: Come up and show us. I'll run the timer for the class to see, but I won't let you see. Start counting.	*James invites a demonstration to help students see what is happening.*
Tammy: one, two, three, four, five, six, seven, eight, nine, ten, eleven, twelve, thirteen, fourteen….slight pause, fifteen, sixteen, seventeen… (*several surprised ohs and ahs*).	
Sydney: See. The timer is already ahead of you. Probably when you get to 30, the timer will be at 40!	*Now the conversation is on a big idea. You can't stop when keeping track of a duration and you can't use longer words. Intervals need to be constant.*
James: Interesting! Who else noticed that? (several hands go up). Did anyone figure out why? Anthony?	
Anthony: I think because you stopped at 14. You can't stop or the timer gets ahead.	
Maia: Oh, I get it! Some words took longer too, like the kid in the story said.	
James: Wow! And Sydney was counting so nicely and trying so hard. So, we can't pause, and we can't say some counting words that take longer than others or the timer gets ahead of us. It's really hard to measure time without a timer, isn't it? I tried, too, and I couldn't do it either.	
Carolina: We tried saying 1, 2, 3, 4, 5, 6, 7, 8, 9, 10 and then doing it again. We did it 3 times. That's 30. It was still hard though. I think we need the timer to be exact.	

Math Journals

At the end of the congress, provide everyone with some further reflective writing time. You might ask students to write about an idea or strategy they thought was particularly powerful or a new idea they are now thinking about. Perhaps ask them to write about why the timer is helpful. Giving students time to articulate their new understandings will also provide you with important information that you can use as formative assessment. Take the journals home again tonight and read over the entries. Comment on them.

Dialoguing in journals can be very powerful to keep thinking going and it is a great way to do assessment and to integrate literacy work with mathematics. Take a pic of the entry as evidence of learning!

Reflections on the Day

Math workshop began today with students looking at the comments they received in their journals, considering the questions and challenges posed, and extending or explaining ideas. They continued deepening their understanding about estimating, measuring, and comparing time differences. The congress helped to solidify and extend everyone's understanding of the measurement of time. Giving children time to review their ideas, to justify their thinking, to extend their thinking to other examples, and to learn from each other's work contributes to the development of these young mathematicians in powerful ways, and the classroom becomes a true mathematics and literacy laboratory.

HOW LONG IS A MINUTE?

The day begins with a minilesson designed to focus discussion on splitting a rectangular bar into fourths and halves to mark minutes and seconds. The minilesson serves also as a foundation for a new investigation: how long is a minute? Students continue the estimating work done on Day One and Two, but with a minute as a new duration.

Day Three Outline

Minilesson: A string of related problems

❖ Measure a strip of adding machine paper with 60 connecting cubes, alternating groups of 5 red and 5 white. Cut it and mark the end on the bottom as 60 seconds. On the top, mark 1 minute.

❖ Provide one number at a time from the provided string of related numbers asking students to determine where to mark it.

❖ Provide discussion until consensus is reached and then mark the seconds below the strip and the minutes above the strip.

Developing the Context

❖ Read part two of *The Timekeepers* (Appendix A).

❖ Send pairs off with materials to make further attempts at estimating, representing, and comparing time, as they did on Days One and Two—but today the duration is one minute.

Supporting the Investigation

❖ As students work, move around and confer. Encourage them to note how close they come to 60 seconds (one minute) and to share their strategies. Support them to measure with the cubes and mark the lengths on the strip of adding machine paper.

Math Journals

❖ Provide quiet time for students to write about the things they have noticed and to reflect.

Materials Needed

Adding machine paper

A line of 60 connecting cubes in alternating groups of 5 red, 5 white

Small Timers showing seconds and minutes (one per pair of students)

The Timekeepers (Appendix A)

Math Journals

Pencils

Minilesson: A string of related problems

String an alternating length of 60 connecting cubes (5 red, 5 white, 5 red, 5 white, etc.) above a strip of adding machine paper. Mark the strip with a line, and on the bottom write 60 seconds. Explain that time can also be measured in minutes, and that 60 seconds is one minute long. Mark one minute at the top as shown in Figure 3.

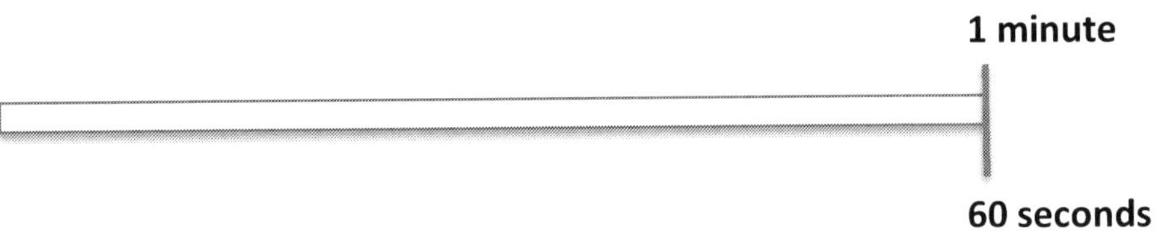

Figure 3: Marking seconds and minutes

Show one number at a time from the provided string of related problems and ask students to determine where the mark should go, each time justifying their reasoning. When consensus is reached make the mark on the bar and mark the seconds underneath. Invite discussion on how much of a minute has passed. Promote discussion on how the minute is two 30-second pieces (one minute cut into 2 equal sections). Mark this above the line as ½ (or as "one half," or just "half").

Tech Tip:

A quick internet search of "download bars" will likely provide you with some nice images to introduce this minilesson.

Ask students if they have ever seen a download bar on a computer and relate it to time duration.

Teacher Tip:

The purpose of cutting the strip to exactly 60, is to provide for the possibility of folding when students suggest that 30 is half, or exactly in the middle. When they say fourths you can fold again, effectively producing 4 equal portions. The intention is not to formally introduce the notation for fractions at this young age, but to support students to understand that the strip of time can be thought of as being cut into equal portions—that the rectangle can be cut into two and four equal shares, described using the words *halves*, *fourths*, and *quarters*, or with phrases like *half of*, *fourth of*, and *quarter of*. You can describe the minute (the whole) as two sections of 30 seconds, or 30 seconds as half of a minute, or the minute as having four sections of 15 seconds, or 15 seconds as a fourth of a minute. The main intent is to focus discussion on how one can think of the minute as the total of equal smaller shares.

The String:

30

15

45

James (the teacher): Ok, here is our strip of time. It is one minute long. Yesterday we tried to estimate how long 30 seconds was. Where would that amount go on this bar? Show me with a "a thumbs up" when you think you know.

Carolina: I used the connecting cubes above and saw 5 red, and 5 white. That's ten. Then another 5 red and 5 white, that's 20. Then another 5 red and 5 white. That's 30.

James: Does everyone agree with Carolina? Should I mark the 30 seconds right here? (*There is lots of agreement, so James makes a vertical line at the end of the 30th cube, down the bar, and writes 30.*) Did anyone find it a different way? Ricardo?

Ricardo: I think the minute is double 30 seconds because I know that double. 30+30 = 60. So, 30 is right in the middle.

James: Oh, that's interesting. How many people know what Ricardo means? Turn to an elbow partner and discuss this. How did Ricardo find the 30? (*After a few minutes of pair talk, James resumes whole group discussion*).

Sydney: He split the bar in half. **30 seconds is halfway.**

James: Whoa! That's an interesting noticing. We have two equal sections? 30 seconds here and 30 seconds there? So, is 30 seconds the same as **half of a minute**?

Sydney: Yes!

James: Wow. Let's mark that, too, then. (*Marks ½ and writes the word "half" on the top of the strip, above the 30 seconds, which is written under the strip effectively using a double bar model*). All right, what about this next number? Where should I mark 15?

Author's notes

Note how the alternating string of connecting cubes supports students to prioritize chunks of fives and tens. This will be helpful in future years as students work to understand how time can be broken up into five minute chunks.

James doesn't just accept answers. He provides discussion on justifications for answers and explores alternative ways of thinking about it as well.

Sydney has noticed an important thing. 30 seconds is halfway to 60 seconds. Note how James paraphrases and uses the language of half of a minute.

James notates ½ but also uses the word, "half." In the conversation there is also discussion on how 30 is in the middle, that there are two equal sections, and that 30+30 = 60.

Developing the Context

Read the next section of *The Timekeepers* (Appendix A, Part Two, stopping at the bottom of page 41.) Invite discussion on the questions: *Why did the timer skip 60? Was it broken? And, what should it say next?* You will likely have a rich discussion here with some students puzzled and wondering if the timer is broken, and others understanding that because 60 seconds and one minute are equal durations, they can be substituted for each other; the timer hasn't skipped a number, it has just substituted one minute for 60 seconds. Similarly, many children may think that after one minute (01:00), the timer will say 2 minutes (02:00) and continue counting minutes accordingly. This is similar to the same error we often see young children make when they count past 100, saying 200 instead of 101; others will defend why the timer will record seconds next (01:01, 01:02…). Provide discussion and reflection but don't try to resolve disagreements. Instead, send them off in pairs with their math journals, pencils, and a timer to work on two tasks:

As you did on the prior days, take turns doing a movement and estimate the time. But today, try to do the movement for exactly one minute. See how close you can come to one minute without looking at the timer. Record how long you actually did the movement for and explain how you found the difference. Which was harder to estimate: 30 seconds or one minute? Why?

Examine what the timer does after one minute. What numbers are changing? Why?

Supporting the Investigation

Move around the room as students work, listening and noting the strategies they are using. It is likely that estimating a duration of one minute will be substantially harder than estimating 30 seconds. Research supports the fact that longer durations are more difficult for people of all ages to estimate. Even if children try counting to sixty, they may struggle to do so at the same rate, and as the numbers increase, the words have more syllables. Some children may solve this dilemma by counting to 30 twice, effectively doing two half-minute durations. Given the minilesson, others may even do 15 seconds 4 times. Celebrate their strategies and support discussion on how they know that 4 quarters of a minute (or 4 fourths) make one whole minute. This can also be a powerful moment to point out how 2 fourths (15+15) equal one half (30 seconds) of a minute if it did not come up previously in the minilesson.

When conferring on the second question (why the timer records seconds again after 01:00), ask students to consider how many seconds the timer will record before it says 2 minutes (02:00) and support them to notice how slowly the minutes change in relation to the seconds.

Math Journals

There will not be a congress on the work of today. Discussion will occur in the journal and will be between you and each student. Towards that aim, provide everyone with enough reflective writing time to explain their individual thinking on the two tasks they explored during the investigation. Just as you would do during writing workshop, move around and support students as they write. Remind them that you will read what they each write and comment back and so it is important that they communicate all their thinking as best they can to help you understand what they mean. Giving students time to articulate their new understandings will also provide you with important information that you can use as formative assessment. Take the journals home again tonight and read over the entries. Comment on them. Dialoguing in journals can be very powerful to keep thinking going and it is a great way to do assessment. Take a pic of the entry as evidence of their math (and literacy) learning and date it.

Reflections on the Day

Today your students had the opportunity to explore time further. They were introduced to the idea that different units of measure can be used to describe durations, and to how smaller units of time (like seconds) add up to longer units (like minutes). They also examined various equivalencies—30 seconds was also half a minute; a fourth of a minute was also 15 seconds; and 4 quarters of a minute made one whole minute. These ideas will provide the foundation for hours to be explored and for time to be read on both digital and analog clocks as hours and half hours—which will be the focus of the next 2 days. Remember to take the journals home tonight to read each one and comment. Document the growth you see on the landscape. If you are using the New Perspectives assessment app, take a picture of children's work and add it to the landscape.

Teacher Note:

If at all possible, it is very helpful to have math workshop in the morning tomorrow, preferably at 9:00. The activity tomorrow (Day Four) invites students to anticipate what they will be doing at various times during the day. It will be a lot more fun as the day progresses to see if students' anticipated events occur when they expected they would. If your normal schedule is to have math workshop in the afternoon, there won't be much time in the school day left, and the activity will be far less powerful.

THE ANALOG CLOCK

Materials Needed

Math Journals

Pencils

Analog Clocks (preferably one class-size, and a class set of individual student clocks from www.Mathrack.com)

One class-size digital clock (showing only hours and minutes. You can likely find one online that can be displayed)

The Timekeepers (Appendix A)

My Day (Appendix B, one copy per student)

Today begins with students reading the comments you left in their journals last night and then a brief conversation on some of their insights is facilitated. Subsequently the analog clock is introduced in a minilesson, and students learn about hours and how 60 minutes equals one hour. With partners, they anticipate what they will likely be doing at each hour and half hour throughout the day, and fill out Appendix B.

Day Four Outline

Math Journals

❖ Pass out journals and allow students time to read over your comments.
❖ Facilitate a conversation on some of the big ideas about measuring time that were addressed in the journals.

Minilesson: Clock Images

❖ Introduce the analog clock and explain that it was made to keep track of hours since it was too hard to estimate really long periods of time, like 60 minutes.
❖ Using the clock, work on a string of clock images comprised of hours and half hours.

Developing the Context

❖ Display Appendix B and provide a brief discussion on what students think they might be doing at the times shown. Then send them off in pairs to write down their guesses.

Supporting the Investigation

❖ Confer with students as they work.
❖ Allow them to check off correct guesses throughout the day and at the end of the day and to total their scores.

Math Journals

Start math workshop by passing out math journals and allowing students time to read through your comments. For those students who may be challenged with the reading of your notes, move around and help them. Then start a conversation on some of the big ideas about time that you noticed students writing about. They had specifically been asked to address the questions of why the timer didn't say 60 seconds and what they thought the next number would be after one minute (01:00). Promote discussion on this and support students to consider the effect of the equivalence of 60 seconds and one minute. Then move the conversation to why after 01:00 the timer read 01:01. Lastly, ask students if they found it harder to judge one minute than they did the 30 seconds. If some say one minute was easier, ask what strategies they used to help them. If, for example, they did 30 seconds twice, or 15 seconds 4 times, provide conversation on the equivalence of 4 quarters (or 4 fourths) to a minute, and 2 halves to the whole.

Minilesson: Clock Images

To set the stage for the minilesson, you can either read Part Three of *The Timekeepers* (Appendix A), or you can just explain (as a transition to the minilesson) that usually it is more difficult for people to estimate long periods of time. And, that is one of the reasons people invented clocks. They measure long periods of time in hours and minutes. 60 minutes make one hour. Display a class-size digital clock with hours and minutes (emphasizing that this is different than the timer that had only minutes and seconds.) Explain that this clock doesn't have seconds; it only shows hours and minutes. Show 1 o'clock (1:00), and then one-thirty (1:30). Next display the class-size analog clock starting at 12 o'clock and move the big hand all the way around stopping at 1 o'clock. Explain that the big hand actually moves much more slowly than you moved it because to go all the way around it takes 60 minutes. Remind students of how long 1 minute was and have them imagine how long it would take for the hand to move 60 minutes. Compare the displays on both clocks when they say 1 o'clock. Remind students that 30 is half of 60, and so when the digital clock says 1:30 it can also be read as half past one, or as an hour and a half. Next, invite students to consider what 1:30 on the analog clock might look like. Provide pair talk. Resume whole group discussion and at an appropriate time in the discussion help students to see that the circle is cut in half when the big hand points to the 6. Allow students to ask questions and then begin the string, using images on the analog clock of the times listed below in the string, and each time asking, *"What time is it?"* Once everyone agrees with the time, write the time in a digital version but also use the language in the string, for example writing and saying 2:30, but also saying half-past two. As you move from one image to another in the string, invite children to talk about what the hands have done. For example, to get to 2:30 from 2:00, the minute hand moves 30 minutes more—half an hour more.

The String:
two o'clock (2:00)
half-past two (2:30)
three o'clock (3:00)
half-past three (3:30)
four o'clock (4:00)

Developing the Context

After the minilesson, display a copy of Appendix B. Invite students to think about what they were doing at some of the earlier times in the day. For example, at 8:00 AM, they may have been on their way to school. At 8:30, they may have been in morning meeting, and at 9:00 you might have been starting math workshop. Record a few of the things there is consensus on, drawing the hands on the clocks to match the digital time written underneath each, and then send students off in pairs to think about what they might be doing at the upcoming times listed on the sheet.

Supporting the Investigation

Don't be alarmed if students guess randomly, for example listing lunch at 3:00! This is to be expected as they do not likely have a good enough sense of time yet to even imagine an hour and they are likely also challenged by just reading the clock. The purpose of this activity is not to assess children's ability to get correct answers. It is only to get them engaged in thinking about time so that as the day continues they notice the time and how the hands are moving, and they think about whether their guess was right, or not. As the day progresses, stop at as many of the designated times listed on Appendix B as possible and bring students' attention to what they are doing. Have them check their sheet and decide if they guessed right, or not. If they did, have them put a check. If they didn't, you can allow them to change it if you want, although this is not necessary. At the end of the day they can total up their checks.

Reflections on the Day

Today your students had the opportunity to further deepen their understanding of time as they used both analog and digital time and recorded their activity at designated intervals. Tomorrow the unit culminates with a matching game, where they have to match digital time with analog time (hours and half hours only).

Although this unit is a short one, and several of your children may still be challenged with telling time and particularly with reading an analog clock correctly, there are activities suggested that you can continue doing to support them even when the unit is over. The activity today of anticipating events and matching them to a time (displayed on a clock) can be done many times, with several versions. The more you do it, the better students will become at thinking of the day in chunks of hours and half hours. You can also have them keep a log of exactly what they do at designated times, and you can send this assignment home as homework. The Appendix is designed in a way that if you copy it you will have 24 hours. This allows children to record the times they were asleep and when they woke up. Doing so, will not only support your students to tell time, it can provide you with insights into what time they went to bed, what they did after school, and even what time they had dinner and breakfast—all of which can sometimes affect the behavior you see at school.

WHAT TIME IS IT?

Today begins with another minilesson using more analog clock images and then a matching game using cards with digital and analog clock faces is introduced. Math workshop ends with the making of a learning scroll—a documentation of the learning and the activities that occurred over the duration of the unit.

Day Five Outline

Minilesson: a string of related problems

❖   Using the clock, work on a string of clock images comprised of hours and half hours, showing one image at a time and inviting discussion.

Developing the Context

❖   Introduce the game *What Time is It?* by modeling with a student how to play in a fishbowl for the rest of the class to see.

❖   Pass out sets of cards to pairs.

Supporting the Investigation

❖   Note students' strategies as they work and encourage discussion on cards that can be matches. This is also a good time to assess, determining which students may still need further work on time, even though the unit is ending.

Building a Learning Scroll

❖   Use children's ideas and samples of their work from throughout the five days of this unit to make a learning scroll of the progression of their thinking about time.

❖   Make obvious on the scroll somewhere the time duration of the work and display it on a bulletin board or in the hallway for reflection.

Materials Needed

A class-size analog clock

Sets of Time Cards for playing the game *What Time is It?* (Appendix C, one set of cards per pair of students)

Sets of Clock Cards for playing the game *What Time is It?* (Appendix D, one set of cards per pair of students)

Sample student work from each activity in the unit

Chart Paper for the Learning Scroll

Markers

Glue sticks

Math Journals

Pencils

Minilesson: Clock Images

Show images on the analog clock (one-at-a-time) of the times listed below in the string, each time asking, *"What time is it?"* Invite discussion and once everyone agrees with the time, write it in a digital version but also use the language in the string (for example writing and saying 2:30, but also saying half-past two). As you move from one image to another in the string, invite children to talk about what the hands have done. For example, to get to 12:30 from 12:00, the minute hand moved 30 minutes—half an hour more.

The String:

twelve o'clock (12:00)

half-past twelve (12:30)

one o'clock (1:00)

three o'clock (3:00)

half-past three (3:30)

half-past four (4:30)

half-past five (5:30)

six o'clock (6:00)

Behind the Numbers

The times have been chosen carefully to support students to consider, not just what the clock says, but to also consider the duration of the time change. The duration of elapsed time from 12:00 to 12:30 is 30 minutes or half an hour. Providing the images consecutively supports students to understand why 12:30 can also be referred to as half-past twelve. By doing 1:00 next, students are challenged to consider how the other half an hour completes a full turn of the minute hand, but also why on a clock 1 comes next, not 13. This is an opportunity to explain that there are only 12 hours on a clock and that midnight is 12 AM and noon is 12 PM. Although military time is expressed as 13:00, it is not advisable to get into this with first graders as it will likely be confusing since 13 is not on the clock. The elapsed time between 1:00 and 3:00 is 2 hours and this provides students with a chance to see that only the hours changed. The next 3 images build hours onto the half hour, until the end of the string, when 30 minutes are needed to get to 6:00. You may be wondering why discussions on elapsed time are suggested here. Telling time is a meaningless activity for students unless they understand what is being measured. An analogy would be asking students to say the number aloud when the numeral is shown, without having any idea of the quantity or even how to count!

Developing the Context

Ask students to form a circle in the meeting area and choose a student to join you in the center to play *What Time is It?* Turn all time cards (Appendix C) face-down. Turn all clock cards (Appendix D) face-up and arrange them in 4 equal rows. Ask, "What time is it?" and invite your playing partner to choose a time card and say it aloud. You must now find a match from the clock cards that are displayed face-up. For example, if the time is 8:00, you must match it with an analog clock image of 8 o'clock. The match is placed to the side with the matched times showing face-up. Now your partner asks, "What time is it?" and you turn over a time card and say it aloud. Play continues until all matches have been made. Play is collaborative with a goal to make as many matches as possible, effectively using all cards on the table. There are 24 possible matches. Once all matches have been made, players work to arrange them in a sequence from 12:00 to 11:30.

Supporting the Investigation

Move around and confer as students play. Note the developing flexibility to read the face of the analog clock. This is also an opportune time to do some formative assessment. If you find some of your children are still quite challenged trying to read the clock face, make a note so that you provide them with more experiences playing the game post the completion of the unit.

Building a Learning Scroll

A learning scroll is a class display—a sort of " socio-historical" wall—documenting the progression of the unit, children's questions, the important ideas constructed over the duration of the unit, samples of students' work, and descriptions of their strategies and ideas, including anecdotes of how students' thinking changed over time. It is a document of the progression and emergence of learning over the past five days. By making this display available for some time, you allow your students to revisit and reflect on all the wonderful ideas and strategies that emerged as they worked throughout the unit and you also provide a look at an even longer time duration—one measured not in hours, but in days.

Use a roll of chart paper and cut out a long length sufficient to cover a bulletin board or a display area in a hallway. Curl and staple the two ends, making a small roll on each end. Staple or tape it to the area to be covered. On the left, begin with a short description of the first activity with a few samples of children's early work and ideas. Some teachers use pictures of the children and cartoon bubbles with quotes of some of the early ideas they had. Selectively pick key pieces of children's work from the five days of the unit (or take pictures of some pages of their journals with their permission) and include brief anecdotal descriptions of their ideas as they worked on activities. Provide documentation of the emerging learning with the pieces you pick. Wherever you can, show the developmental emergence of ideas on the landscape in the Overview. Display the scroll and ask children to look at it and reflect with you on all the wonderful ideas they constructed over the course of this unit. Keep it displayed for several weeks so that they can revisit again and again the notion of time as a measured duration.

Reflections on the Unit

Absolute, true, and mathematical time, in and of itself and of its own nature, without reference to anything external, flows uniformly and by another name is called duration. Relative, apparent, and common time is any sensible and external measure (precise or imprecise) of duration by means of motion; such as a measure—for example, an hour, a day, a month, a year—is commonly used instead of true time.

Sir Isaac Newton

In this unit, your children had opportunities to experience duration and to extract chunks of the duration with beginnings and ends. They were challenged to determine ways to measure these time durations and initially used counting—only to determine that this might not be the best way to measure time. As they tried out timers and clocks, both digital and analog, they had opportunities to explore how consistent standard intervals were needed to compare durations. With timers, they used seconds and minutes, and represented durations and their estimates on duration bars—a contextual model that serves as a precursor to an open number line model and a timeline. These models eventually become tools for thinking. With clocks, students experienced how units can be added and decomposed into equal parts and how these parts could be expressed in many ways, specifically how 30 minutes can also be expressed as half an hour.

The focus of this unit has been not just on the "telling of time" but on the development of an *understanding* of time and the many ways to measure it. Along the way, several big ideas about the measurement of time were constructed: to compare durations, a standard unit is needed; larger units can encompass (and be decomposed into) smaller units; durations can be added and subtracted; durations can be cut into equal (fractional) portions; and small units can be unitized into bigger units (for example 60 minutes can be unitized into 1 hour.) And now, most likely, you are witnessing several of your children using equivalent portions, unitizing them, and substituting and exchanging different representations with meaning, for example calling 1½ hours, half-past-one, 1:30, and maybe even 90 minutes.

Others may still be challenged. This is to be expected; this unit was a short one. It ended however with a game that you can use over and over throughout the year, and an activity (Day Four) that you can also use frequently as a routine. You can also do minilessons with clock images with small groups for further support. Continue with these activities. Development takes time. Journey with your children, supporting their steps along the way with patience. Children, when they are respected as young mathematicians at work, come to see beauty all around them as they mathematize their lived worlds with mathematical creations based on their own meaning-making.

Tamika and Tanisha are best friends. They live next door to each other and have played together every day since they were babies. And now, they are in the same class together in school! Mrs. Washington is their teacher and she is always finding fun math problems for them to do. "Investigations," Mrs. Washington calls them.

One day Mrs. Washington said, "Let's investigate time!"

Tamika turned to Tanisha with a puzzled look and said, "Huh? What does she mean by that? How do you investigate time?" Tanisha just shrugged her shoulders. She couldn't imagine what Mrs. Washington meant either.

"What is time?" Mrs. Washington asked.

"It takes a long time when you are sitting in a car on a long trip," Elijah said. "When we visit my grandma, my mom says it takes two hours to get there!"

"My mom always looks at her watch when she talks about time," Jayden offered. "Then she says, hurry up and get ready or we are going to be late. We are running out of time!"

Tamika remembered something she had heard her mom say. "When my mom has to work on weekends," Tamika put forth shyly, "she always says, 'Oh well, time is money'."

"Those are all good ideas," Mrs. Washington said. "Do you think time can be measured?"

"Do you mean like we do with cubes to see how long something is?" Jayden asked with a puzzled look.

"Well, for example, what if I stand up?" Mrs. Washington asked. "You could measure how tall I am with a tower of cubes, right?"

Tamika thought to herself, "Sure, but what does that have to do with time? How could you measure time with cubes?"

Mrs. Washington went on, "What if we start counting when I stand up and keep counting until I sit down? Let's try that."

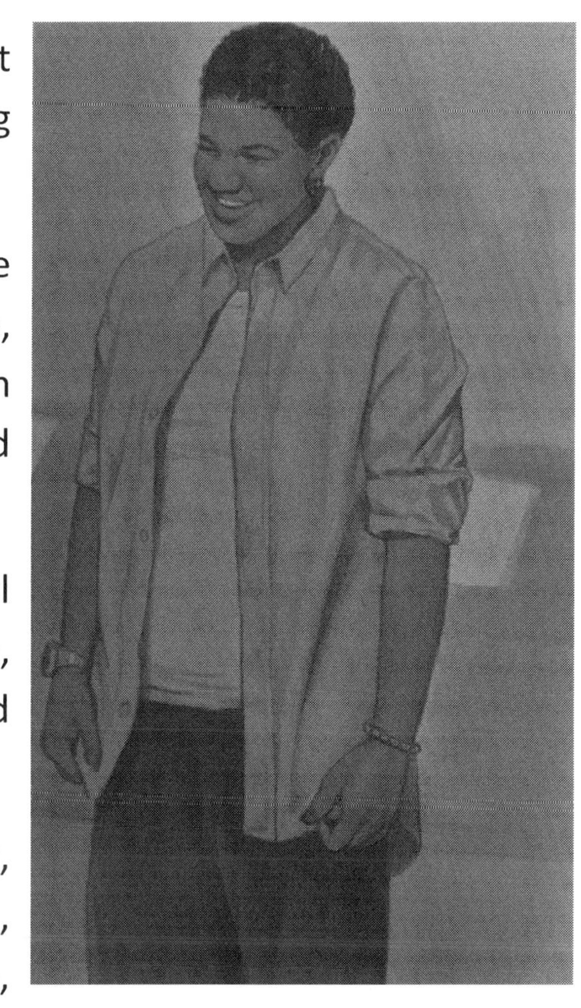

Mrs. Washington stood up and everyone started counting, "One, two, three, four, five, six, seven, eight, nine, ten." Mrs. Washington promptly sat down when she heard ten, and everyone stopped counting.

"Ok, so the time I stood took 10 counts. I'll write that down. Now let's try it again, ready?" Mrs. Washington stood up and everyone started counting again.

"One, two, three, four, five, six, seven, eight, nine, ten, eleven, twelve, thirteen, fourteen, fifteen, sixteen, seventeen, eighteen, nineteen, twenty, twenty-one, twenty-two, twenty-three, twenty-four, twenty-five, twenty-six, twenty-seven." Mrs. Washington sat down. Some kids kept counting though.

"Stop!" Tanisha said. "She sat down! She sat down when we said twenty-seven!"

Tamika giggled because some kids were still counting.

"Ok, let's write that down, too." Mrs. Washington said. "So, the first time I was standing, it was for 10 counts, and the second time it was for 27 counts. Can we tell which time was the longest?

Jayden raised his hand. "The last time was longer. More than twice as long!" he said, stretching his hands out to show 10 first and then stretching them way out to show 27. He wanted to show how the second time compared to the first time. It was more than double!

"We can mark that on a strip like we do with numbers and make a timeline," Tamika said, and she got up and marked the 10. "And then I can mark the 27 and we can see how the times compare."

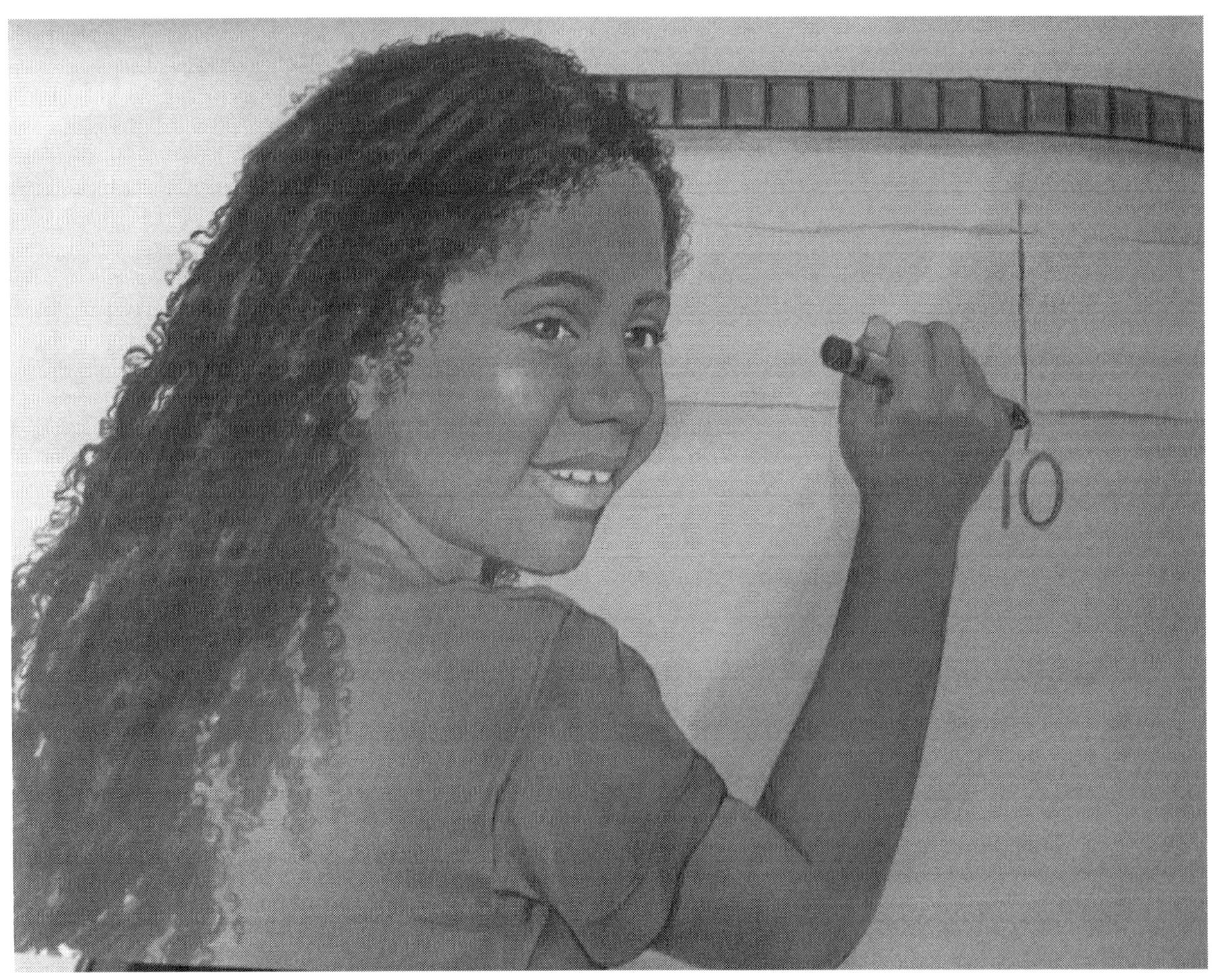

"But it takes longer to say some of the words," pointed out Elijah. "When we say one, it's a lot shorter than saying twenty-seven. I don't think counting is a good way."

"That's a big thing you just said, Elijah. The beats all need to be the same to compare the times, don't they?" Elijah beamed when Mrs. Washington said, "a big thing." He liked that she thought he had said something big; he felt proud. Mrs. Washington gave him a warm smile in acknowledgement, and then she continued with an example to show what Elijah meant, "When we try to measure really long times we would have to say numbers like one million, three-hundred twenty-four thousand, eight-hundred sixty-seven, and then…, one million, three-hundred twenty-four thousand, eight-hundred sixty-eight. It would take us so long to say the words we couldn't compare it to saying just one, two... could we? There are some timekeeping tools we could explore that might help to solve this problem, though. I have a timer we could use to keep time. Here is what it looks like."

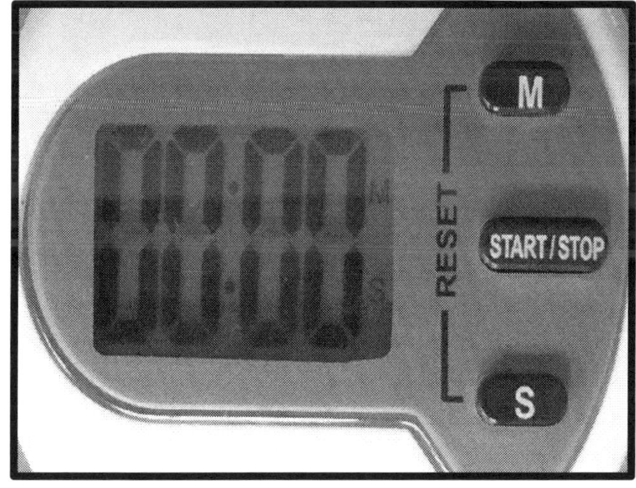

"Why does it have all those zeros on it?" Tanisha asked.

"It gets set to start at 00 minutes and 00 seconds," explained Mrs. Washington. "Elijah, come stand up for awhile like I did and we'll time you and we can see what the numbers on the timer do."

Elijah stood up and Mrs. Washington started the timer by pressing start. The seconds were being counted. Elijah wasn't sure when to sit down. When would 30 seconds be up? He couldn't see the timer because Mrs. Washington was only letting the class see it. He finally sat down, and Mrs. Washington showed him what the timer said. It said, 00:42.

"You stood for 42 seconds," Mrs. Washington said to Elijah. "Did you stand too long, or not long enough?"

Elijah thought to himself, "42 comes after 30." Aloud he said, "Too long! Can I try again?"

"Let's record what happened, first," Mrs. Washington said. She drew a mark on the strip just like Tamika had done earlier. She used the cubes to help her find 30 and then she asked, "Where should I mark 42 seconds?"

"Ten more gets you to 40," Tamika began. "And then 2 more." Mrs. Washington followed Tamika's directions and marked the 42.

"You did stand too long, Elijah," Mrs. Washington said with a smile. "It is hard to judge time, isn't it? How many extra seconds did you do?"

"That's a hard question," Elijah thought to himself. But then he realized that he could use what Tamika had said. 10 + 2 = 12. He had stood 12 seconds too long.

 and begin the investigation on Day 1

Part Two: Start Here for the Investigation on Day Three.

Tamika looked at the timer quizzically, and then at Mrs. Washington. "What are the other numbers for, the ones that didn't change?" she asked.

"Those are the minutes," replied Mrs. Washington. "A minute is much longer than a second. It takes 60 seconds to make a minute."

"A minute is twice as long as 30 seconds!" exclaimed Elijah.

"Wow! Another big idea! How did you know that, Elijah?"

"Because I know 30+30 = 60." Elijah explained. "It's a double I know."

Mrs. Washington smiled, "That's great, Elijah. It really helps to know doubles, because now we also know that 30 seconds is half of a minute." Elijah beamed. He hadn't thought of it that way, but Mrs. Washington was right. If 30+30 made 60, then 30 was half of a minute because the two halves would make one whole minute.

"Let's watch the timer to see what happens to the numbers when we do 60 seconds," Mrs. Washington said. She started the timer and the numbers for the seconds started changing. They went, 00:01, 00:02, 00:03, 00:04….

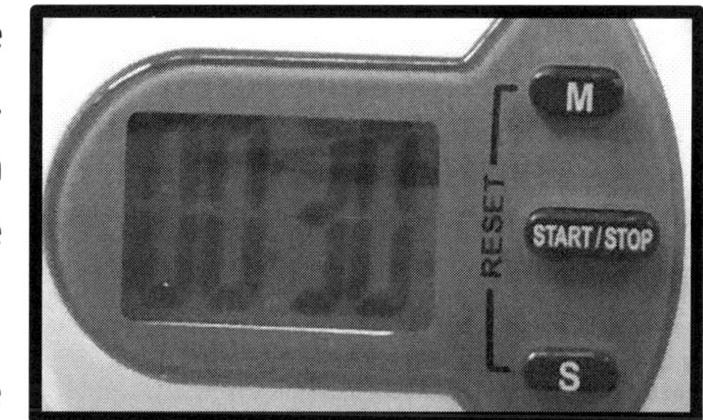

Soon the timer said 30 seconds and the other numbers still hadn't changed yet. "But, we're halfway there," Elijah exclaimed with glee. "30 seconds more and we'll be at a minute!"

The timer kept going and everyone started counting with it, "31, 32, 33, 34, 35, 36, 37, 38, 39, 40, 41, 42….."

"Forty-two. That's the number of seconds I did before," thought Elijah. "I wonder how many seconds more I needed to do to make one minute?"

[*Stop here for a brief discussion on Elijah's question, and then go on with the story.*]

"42…. So, I need 8 more seconds to get to 50, and then 10 more to get to 60. And, 60 seconds is one minute. Wow. I almost did one minute. I just needed 18 seconds more!" Elijah was proud of himself for solving this. Now he understood how time could be measured!

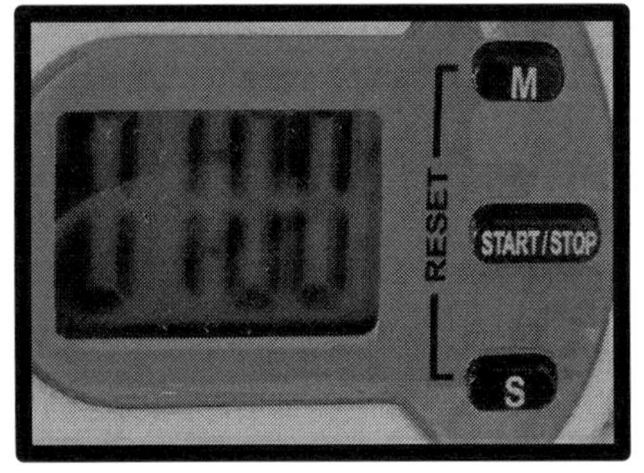

Soon the timer was on 59 seconds. Everyone knew what would come next, and they all said loudly, "60!" But the timer didn't say 60. It said, 01:00!

Why did it skip 60? Was it broken? And, what would it say next?

 and begin the investigation on Day 3

Start Here for the Investigation on Day Four.

"One minute is the same thing as 60 seconds, so it recorded the minute instead. And now, the timer shows seconds again. It shows 01:01, then 01:02, and it keeps going like that," Mrs. Washington explained. "When it says 01:59, the next number is 02:00. Two minutes! And the longer the time period gets, the harder it is to estimate it! That's why now we have clocks to help us keep track of time."

* * *

A very long time ago, people didn't have clocks. They tried to keep track of time with the sun. They watched when it came up in the morning and when it went down in the evening. That helped them count days and nights, but it didn't help too much during the day. Imagine if people wanted to tell friends when to meet up and they didn't have a clock! People would come at all different times!

To help solve this problem, people used big stones and sticks and looked at the shadows. Depending on where the sun was in the sky and how it shone on the stone, the shadow moved. But you had to be in the field to watch the shadows. Some people made small sundials for their yards out of metal, but one day someone had a big idea! They made a water clock. Water would drip into a bucket until it was full, and then it would tip over, emptying the water, and a bell would ring. Then the bucket would right itself and start filling again. Now people could say to their friends, 'I'll meet you under the bell tower when the bell rings 3 times!

But now we have better clocks and keeping track of time is much easier.

This clock measures seconds with the silver hand. It turns fairly quickly because seconds go by quickly. When 60 seconds have passed, the long black hand moves one minute. Look closely and you will see that it is on the one minute mark. When the minute hand has turned 60 minutes, all the way around, the short hand moves one hour. An hour is a pretty long time. It is 60 minutes! This clock says one minute past one o'clock. When the long black hand finishes moving all the way around, it will point to the 12, and the little hand will point to the 2, and the clock will then say 2 o'clock."

and begin the investigation on Day Four

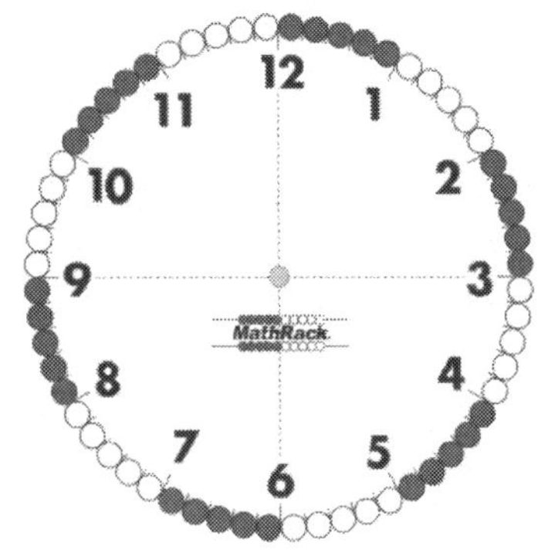

8:00 ____

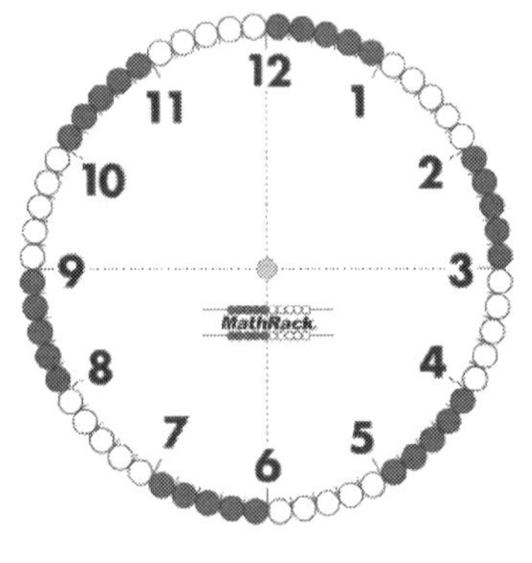

8:30 ____

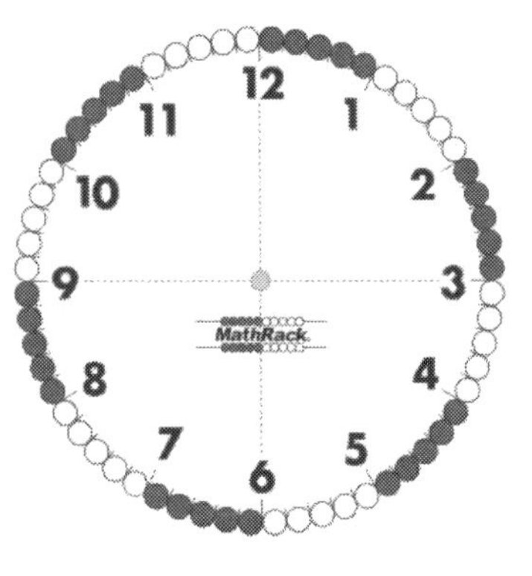

9:00 ____

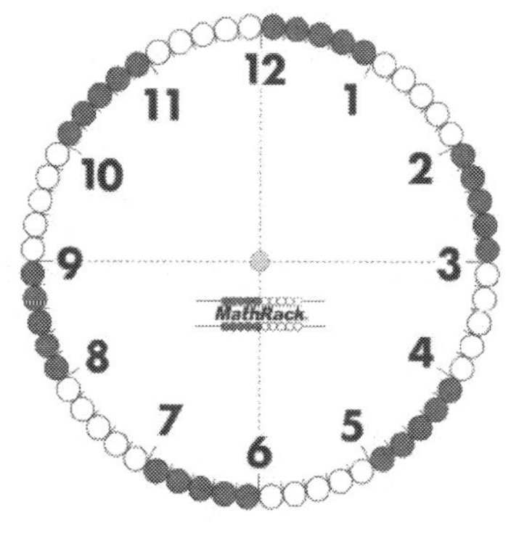

9:30 ____

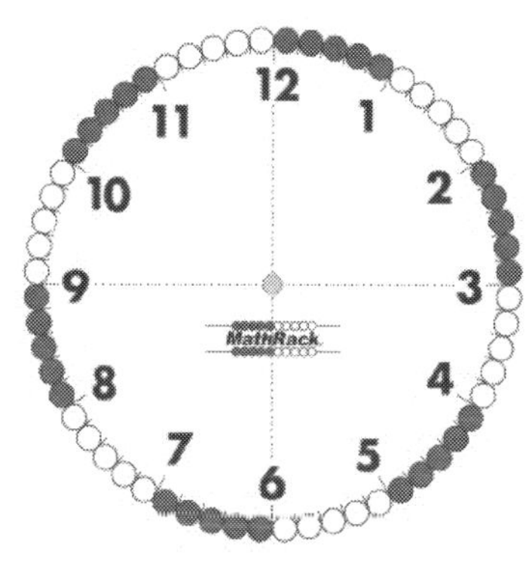

10:00 ____

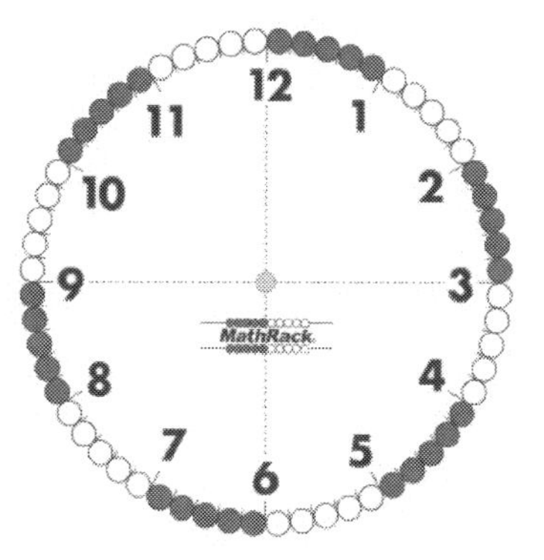

10:30 ____

11:00 ____

11:30 ____

12:00 ____

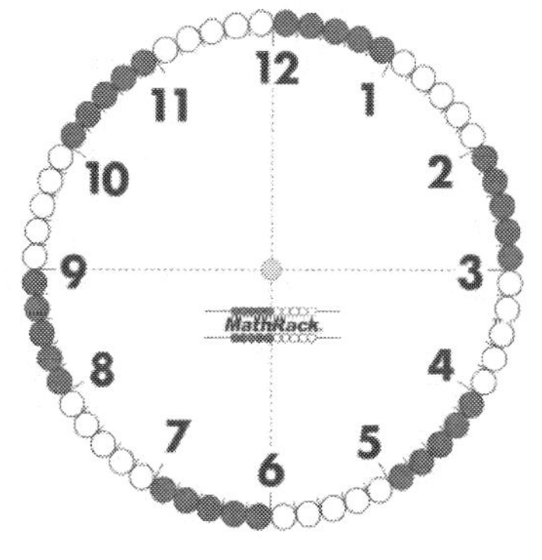

12:30 ____

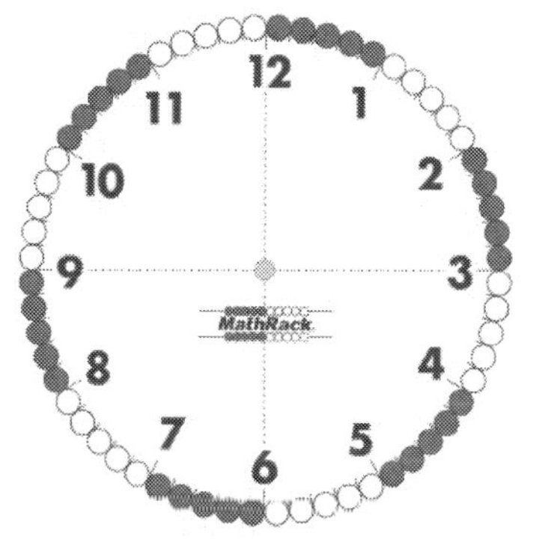

1:00 ____

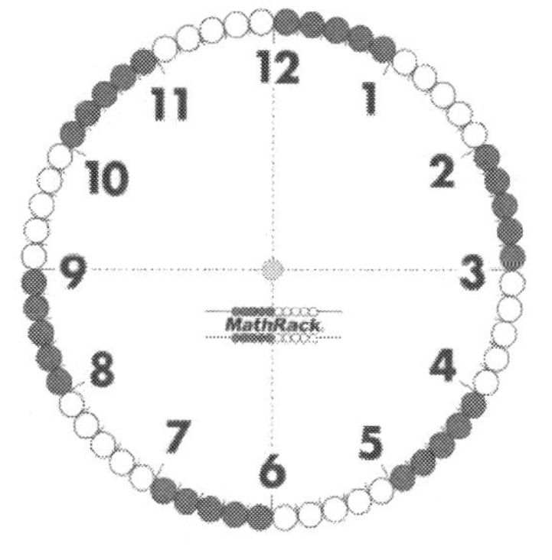

1:30 ____

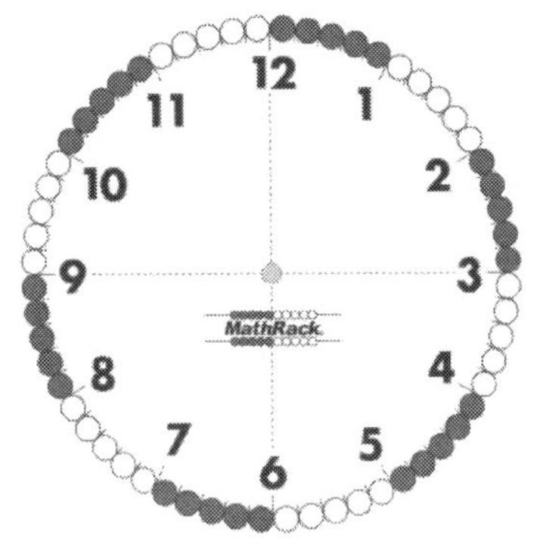

2:00 ____

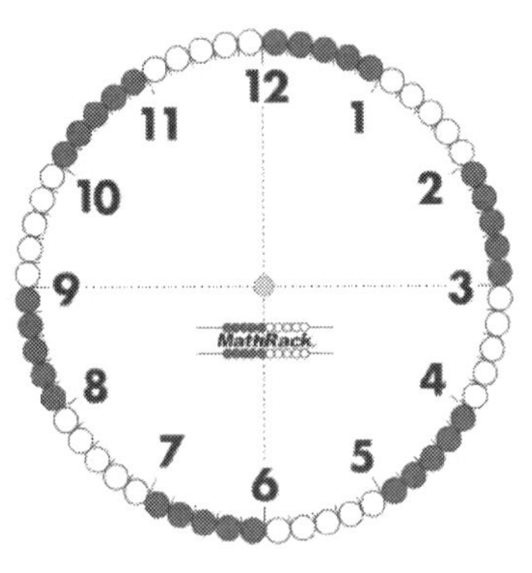

2:30 ____

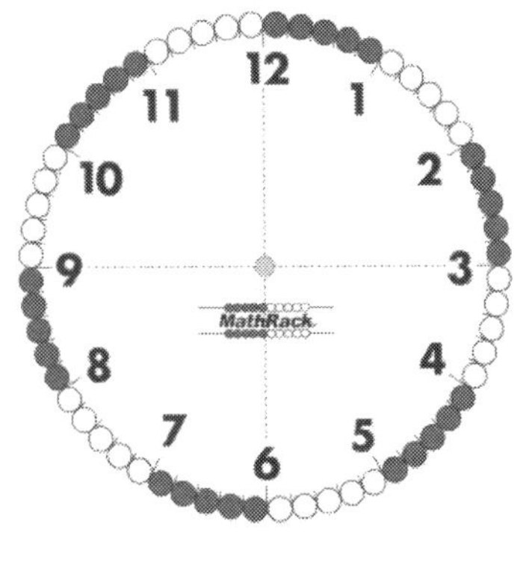

3:00 ____

3:30 _______________________________________

4:00 _______________________________________

4:30 _______________________________________

5:00 ____

5:30 ____

6:00 ____

6:30 ____

7:00 ____

7:30 ____

Set-up: All 24 time cards are shuffled and placed in a face-down pile in the center of the playing area. All 24 clock cards are placed face-up in 4 equal rows.

Game Play:

- ❖ Player One asks, "What time is it?" thereby inviting the playing partner (Player Two) to choose a time card and say it aloud.
- ❖ Player One must now find a match from the clock cards that are displayed face-up. For example, if the time card is 8:00, it is matched with an analog clock image of 8 o'clock. The match is placed to the side with the matched cards showing face-up.
- ❖ Turns alternate, so now Player Two asks, "What time is it?" and Player One turns over a time card and says it aloud. Player Two finds a matching clock card.
- ❖ Play continues until all matches have been made.
- ❖ Play is collaborative with players helping each other as needed. The goal is to make as many matches as possible, effectively using all cards on the table. There are 24 possible matches. Players use small individual clocks to help them.
- ❖ Once all matches have been made, players work to arrange them in a sequence from 12:00 to 11:30.

12:00	**12:30**	**1:00**	**1:30**
2:00	**2:30**	**3:00**	**3:30**
4:00	**4:30**	**5:00**	**5:30**
6:00	**6:30**	**7:00**	**7:30**
8:00	**8:30**	**9:00**	**9:30**
10:00	**10:30**	**11:00**	**11:30**

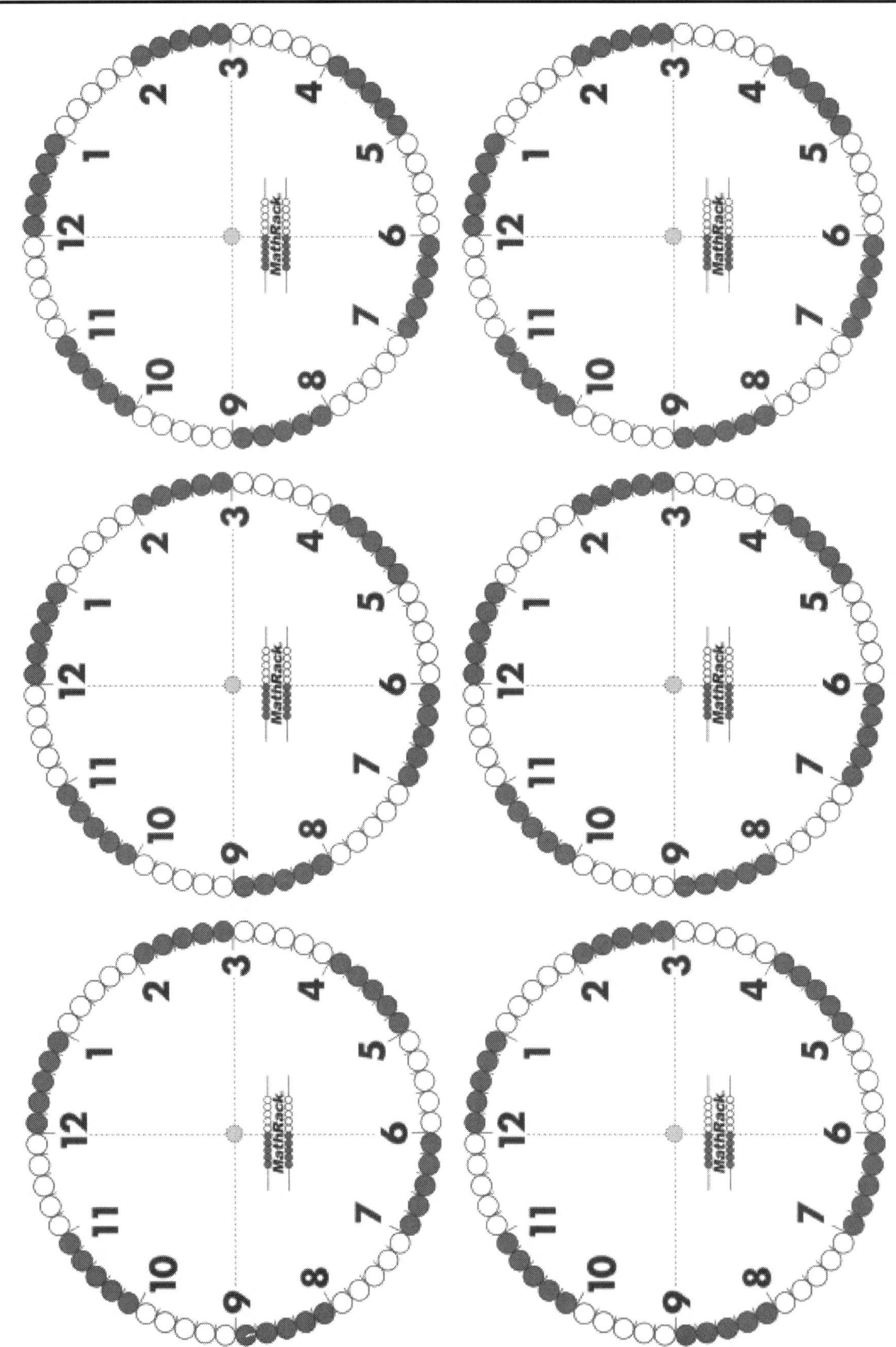

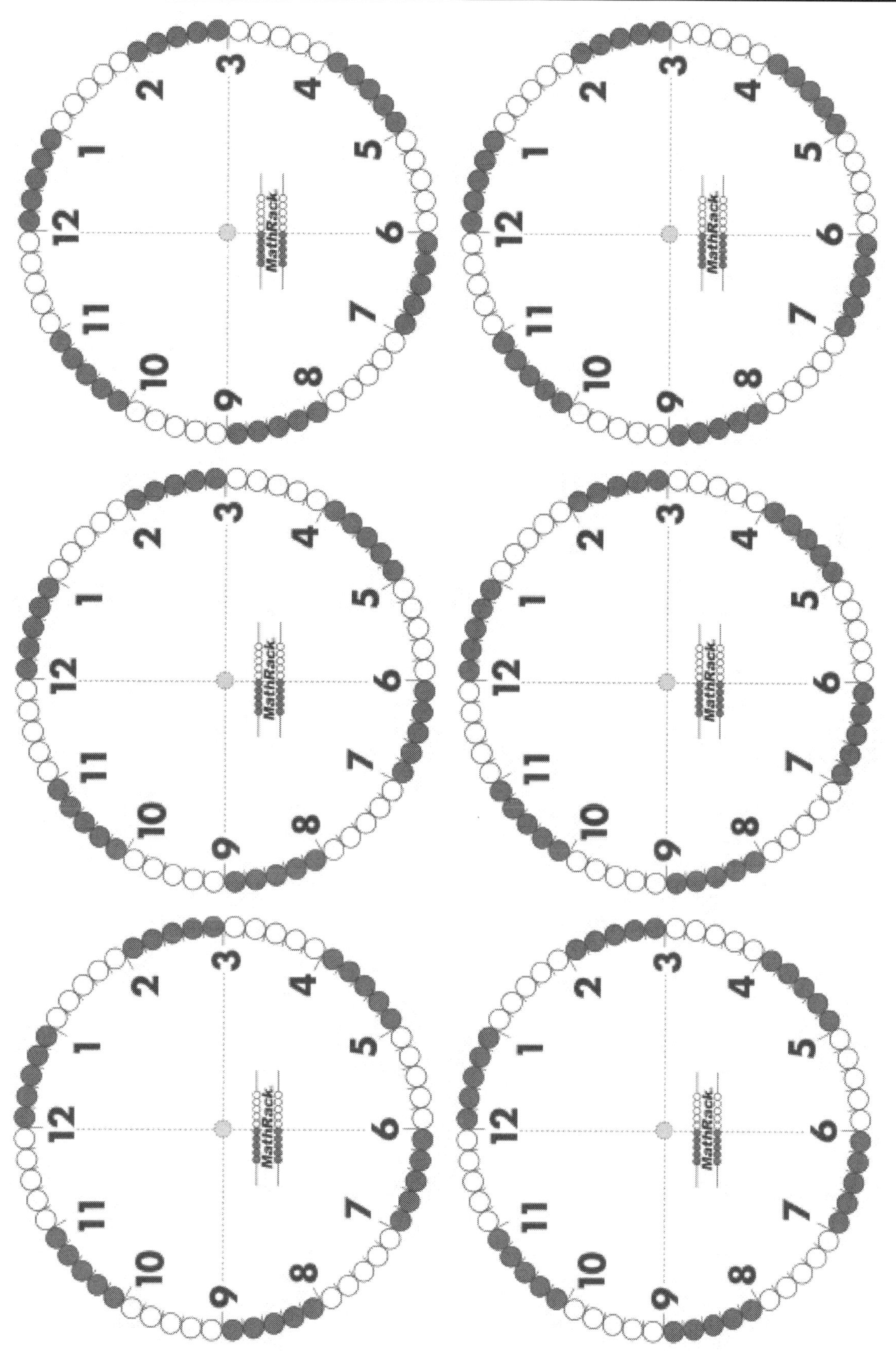

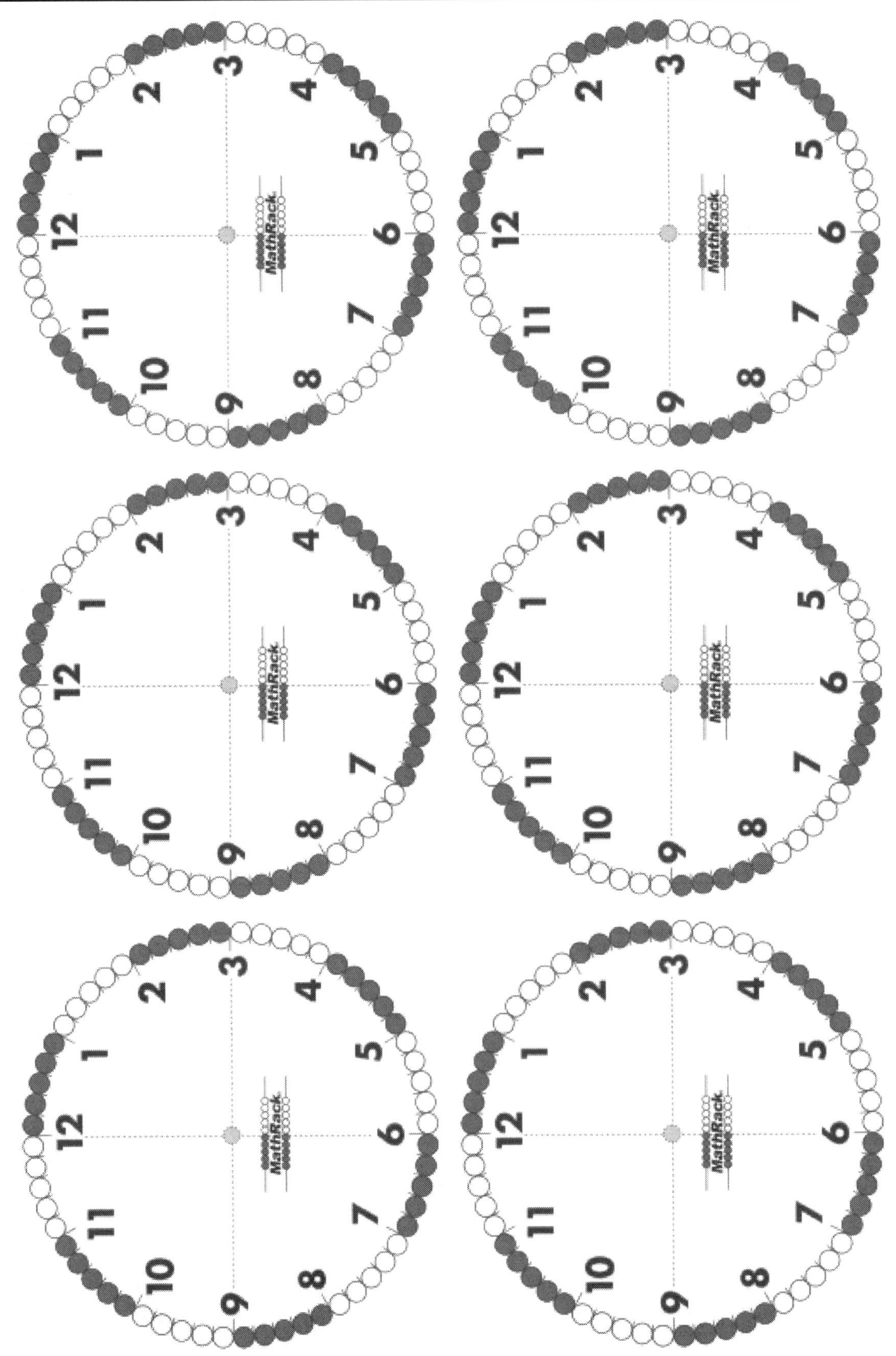

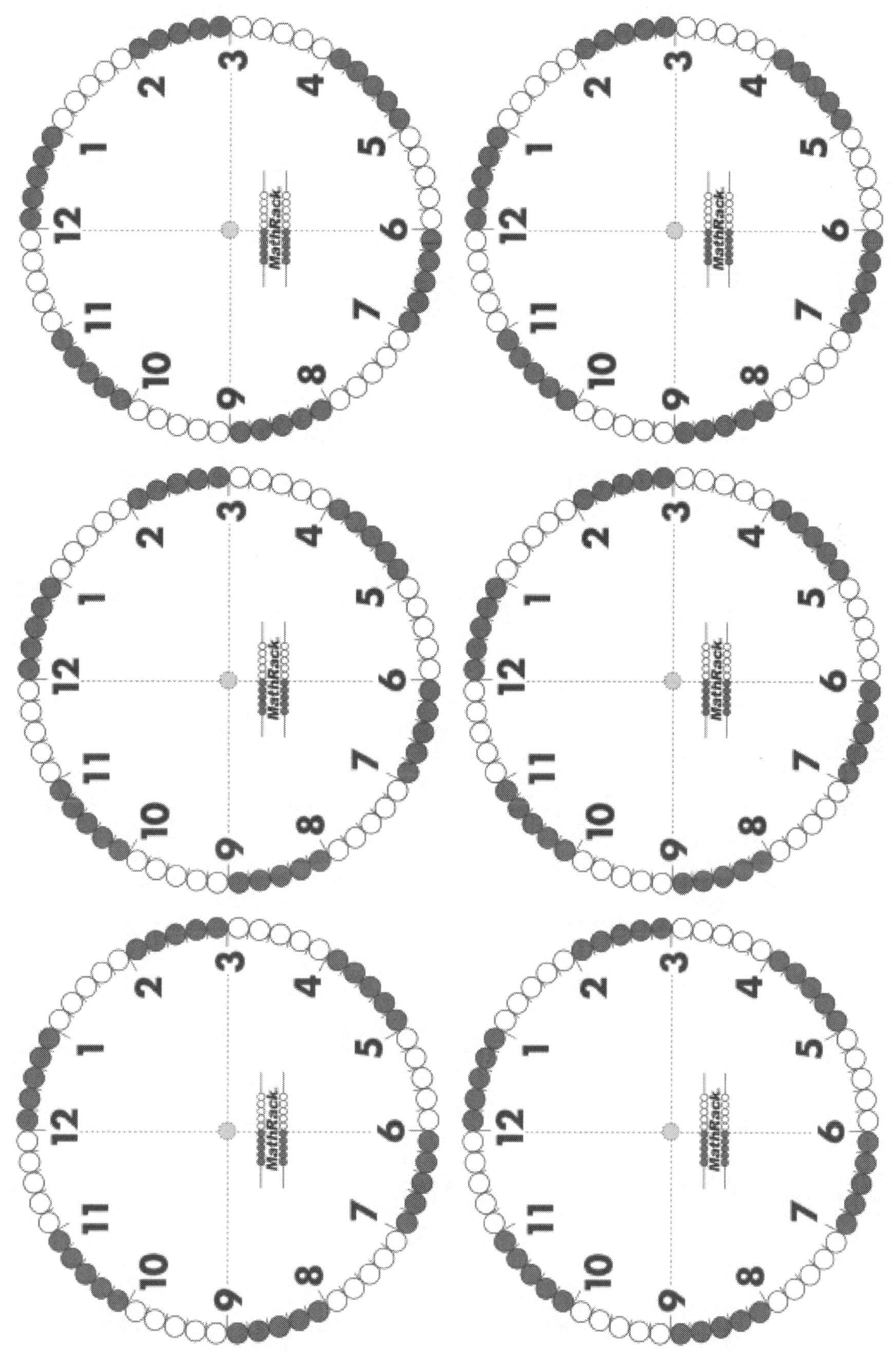

Made in the USA
Monee, IL
12 June 2023

35530292R00033